# BILLY GRAHAM

Evangelistic Association

*Always* Good News.

Dear Friend,

I am pleased to send you this copy of *Discovering the Power of the Cross of Christ* by the well-known English preacher Charles Spurgeon. During the 1800s, his ministry touched hundreds of thousands of lives, and today his spiritual insights continue to inspire countless more.

I believe you will be blessed by Spurgeon's passion to exalt Jesus Christ and his ability to express profound scriptural truths in simple language. This book will remind you of the amazing love and grace God lavished on us through the cross and how you can become more like Jesus through the power of His resurrection. I pray you will discover a greater love for the One who "*is able to save completely those who come to God through him, because he always lives to intercede for them*" (Hebrews 7:25, NIV).

For more than 60 years, the Billy Graham Evangelistic Association has worked to take the Good News of Jesus Christ throughout the world by every effective means available, and I'm excited about what God will do in the years ahead.

We would appreciate knowing how our ministry has touched your life. May God richly bless you.

Sincerely,

Franklin Graham
President

If you would like to know more about our ministry, please contact us:

**IN THE U.S.:**
Billy Graham Evangelistic Association
1 Billy Graham Parkway
Charlotte, NC 28201-0001
billygraham.org
info@bgea.org
Toll-free: 1-877-247-2426

**IN CANADA:**
Billy Graham Evangelistic
    Association of Canada
20 Hopewell Way NE
Calgary, AB T3J 5H5
billygraham.ca
Toll-free: 1-888-393-0003

# STEPS TO PEACE WITH GOD

### 1.  RECOGNIZE GOD'S PLAN—PEACE AND LIFE

The message in this book stresses that
God loves you and wants you
to experience His peace and life.

The BIBLE says ... For God loved the
world so much that He gave His only Son,
so that everyone who believes in Him may
not die but have eternal life. John 3:16

### 2.  REALIZE OUR PROBLEM—SEPARATION FROM GOD

People choose to disobey God and go
their own way. This results in
separation from God.

The BIBLE says ... Everyone has sinned
and is far away from God's saving
presence. Romans 3:23

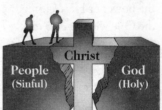

### 3.  RESPOND TO GOD'S REMEDY—THE CROSS OF CHRIST

God sent His Son to bridge the gap. Christ
did this by paying the penalty of our sins
when He died on the cross and rose from
the grave.

The BIBLE says ... But God has shown
us how much He loves us—it was while we
were still sinners that Christ died for us!
Romans 5:8

### 4.  RECEIVE GOD'S SON—LORD AND SAVIOR

You cross the bridge into God's family
when you ask Christ to come into your life.

The BIBLE says ... Some, however, did
receive Him and believed in Him; so He
gave them the right to become God's
children. John 1:12

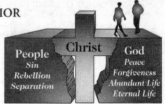

**THE INVITATION IS TO:**
REPENT (turn from your sins), ASK for God's forgiveness, and by faith RECEIVE
Jesus Christ into your heart and life and follow Him in obedience as your Lord
and Savior.

**PRAYER OF COMMITMENT**
"Dear Lord Jesus, I know that I am a sinner, and I ask for Your forgiveness. I believe
You died for my sins and rose from the dead. I turn from my sins and invite You to
come into my heart and life. I want to trust and follow You as my Lord and Savior.
In Your Name, Amen."

*If you are committing your life to Christ, please let us know!*

Billy Graham Evangelistic Association
1 Billy Graham Parkway, Charlotte, NC 28201-0001
1-877-2GRAHAM (1-877-247-2426)
billygraham.org/Commitment

# CHARLES SPURGEON

❖

## DISCOVERING THE POWER OF THE CROSS OF CHRIST

❖

### COMPILED AND EDITED BY
# LANCE WUBBELS

This *Billy Graham Library Selection* is published by the
Billy Graham Evangelistic Association with
permission from Emerald Books.

Scripture quotations are taken from the King James Version of the Bible.

A *Billy Graham Library Selection* designates materials that are appropriate for a well-rounded collection of quality Christian literature, including both classic and contemporary reading and reference materials.

This *Billy Graham Library Selection* is published by the Billy Graham Evangelistic Association with permission from Emerald Books.

**The Power of the Cross of Christ**
©1995
Lance C. Wubbels

Published by Emerald Books
P.O. Box 635
Lynnwood, WA 98046

ISBN: 978-1-59328-309-4
Previous ISBN: 1-883002-16-8

**Printed in the United States of America.**

# About the Author

CHARLES HADDON SPURGEON (1834–1892) was the remarkable British "Boy Preacher of the Fens" who became one of the truly greatest preachers of all time. Coming from a flourishing country pastorate in 1854, he accepted a call to pastor London's New Park Street Chapel. This building soon proved too small and so work on Spurgeon's Metropolitan Tabernacle was begun in 1859. Meanwhile his weekly sermons were being printed and having a remarkable sale—25,000 copies every week in 1865 and translated into more than twenty languages.

Spurgeon built the Metropolitan Tabernacle into a congregation of over 6,000 and added well over 14,000 members during his thirty-eight-year London ministry. The combination of his clear voice, his mastery of language, his sure grasp of Scripture, and a deep love for Christ produced some of the noblest preaching of any age. An astounding 3,561 sermons have been preserved in sixty-three volumes, *The New Park Street Pulpit* and *The Metropolitan Tabernacle Pulpit,* from which the chapters of this book have been selected and edited.

During his lifetime, Spurgeon is estimated to have preached to 10,000,000 people. He remains history's most widely read preacher. There is more available material written by Spurgeon than by any other Christian author, living or dead. His sixty-three volumes of sermons stand as the largest set of books by a single author in the history of Christianity, comprising the equivalent to the twenty-seven volumes of the ninth edition of the *Encyclopedia Britannica*.

# About the Editor

LANCE WUBBELS is the vice president of literary development at Koechel Peterson & Associates, a Minneapolis-based design firm, and Bronze Bow Publishing. Before joining Koechel Peterson, he served for eighteen years as managing editor at Bethany House Publishers and taught biblical courses at Bethany College of Missions in Bloomington, Minnesota.

His interest in the writings of Charles Spurgeon began while doing research on an editorial project that required extensive reading of Spurgeon's sermons. He discovered a wealth of sermon classics that are filled with practical, biblical insight for every believer and written in a timeless manner that makes them as relevant today as the day they were spoken. His desire is to present Spurgeon's writings in a way that allows one of the greatest preachers of all time to enrich believers' lives.

Wubbels has authored several fiction and nonfiction books, including the best-selling gift books with Hallmark, *If Only I Knew, Dance While You Can, I Wish for You,* and *Each Day a New Beginning.* He has published three gift books with Inspired Faith, *Jesus, the Ultimate Gift, A Time for Prayer,* and *To a Child Love Is Spelled T-I-M-E,* which won a 2005 Gold Medallion award from the Evangelical Christian Publishers Association. His novel, *One Small Miracle,* won an Angel Award, and his 365-day devotional, *In His Presence,* also won a Gold Medallion award.

# Contents

## CHARLES SPURGEON
## CHRISTIAN LIVING CLASSICS

*The Power of Christ's Miracles*

*The Power of Christ's Prayer Life*

*The Power of Christ's Second Coming*

*The Power of Christ's Tears*

*The Power of Christ the Warrior*

*The Power of the Cross of Christ*

*The Power of Prayer in a Believer's Life*

*Spiritual Warfare in a Believer's Life*

*What the Holy Spirit Does in a Believer's Life*

## F. B. MEYER
## CHRISTIAN LIVING CLASSICS

*The Life of Paul*

*The Life of David*

*The Life of Joseph*

**FOR MORE INSPIRING TITLES,** visit
**www.ywampublishing.com**

# Introduction

Spanning nearly four decades, Charles Spurgeon's remarkable pastoral and evangelistic ministry in the city of London during the 1800s built the Metropolitan Tabernacle into the world's largest independent congregation. No building seemed big enough to house all those who wanted to hear the passionate biblical expositor who spoke the language of the common people and met them at the point of their deepest need.

As one of the greatest expository preachers and powerful evangelists of all time, Spurgeon credited his amazing success in the ministry to the fact that he remained absolutely faithful to the biblical gospel. This was how he described it: "If I had preached any other than the doctrine of Christ crucified, I should years ago have scattered my audience to the winds of heaven. But the old theme is always new, always fresh, always attractive. Preach Jesus Christ. That is the recipe for catching men's ears and laying hold upon men's hearts. The name of Jesus is to man's heart that most mighty of charms. Ring out the name of Jesus; it is the sweetest carol ever sung. There is about Calvary and its infinite stoop of divine love a power that never dies out and never will while the world stands."

At the core of Spurgeon's preaching was the work of Jesus Christ in His life, death, and resurrection, and it is from this great treasury of messages that we draw the chapters of this book. His messages on the cross of Christ resonate with the amazing wonder of our reconciliation to God, and there is no aspect of the cross that misses his watchful eye. A short quote of Spurgeon's commentary on the three hours of darkness that surrounded the cross give an idea of why these messages are so passionate: "There must be great teaching in this darkness, for when we come so near the cross, which is the center of history, every event is full of meaning. Light will come out of this darkness. I love to feel the solemnity of the three hours of death-shade and to sit down therein and meditate, with no companion but the august Sufferer, around whom that darkness lowered."

But while Spurgeon provides superlative glimpses into our Lord's passion, there is nothing speculative or ethereal about how he saw the cross of Christ impacting the life of a believer. He was thoroughly convinced that "the doctrine of the precious blood, when it gets into the heart, drives error out of it and sets up the throne of truth." He says in another place: "I have chosen this subject that it may help the children of God to understand a little of their infinite obligations to their redeeming Lord. You shall measure the height of His love, if it is ever measured, by the depth of His grief, if that can ever be known. See with what a price He has redeemed us from the curse of the law! As you see this, say to yourself: What manner of people should we be? What measure of love should we return to One who bore the utmost penalty, that we might be delivered from the wrath to come?"

He brings the power of redemption right to our doorstep and asks us: "Do you roll sin under your tongue as a sweet morsel and then come to God's house on Sunday morning and think to worship Him? Worship Him! Worship Him, with sin indulged in your life! If I had a dear brother who had been murdered, what would you think of me if I valued the knife that had been crimsoned with his blood?...Sin murdered Christ; will you be a friend to it? Sin pierced the heart of the Incarnate God; can you love it? Oh, that there was an abyss as deep as Christ's misery, that I might at once hurl this dagger of sin into its depths, whence it might never be brought to light again! Begone, O sin! You are banished from the heart where Jesus reigns!"

Well over one hundred years have gone by since Spurgeon's voice echoed through his great London church, but time has in no way diminished the powerful effect of Spurgeon's words. Come with Charles Spurgeon and glimpse the cross of Christ as he saw it. Listen as he describes Christ's agony in the Garden of Gethsemane, the suffering of Christ on the cross, the powerful words spoken from the cross, and finally the death of Christ. Life-changing messages await you.

Careful editing has helped to sharpen the focus of these sermons while retaining the authentic and timeless flavor they undoubtedly bring.

*But herein is a wonderful thing. The Lord Jesus has lost no influence by having been hanged upon the tree. Rather, it is because of His shameful death that He is able to draw all men unto Himself. His glory rises from His humiliation; His adorable conquest from His ignominious death. When He "became obedient unto death, even the death of the cross" (Phil. 2:8), shame cast no shame upon His cause but gilded it with glory. Christ's death of weakness threw no weakness into Christianity, but rather it is the right arm of her power. By the sign of suffering unto death, the Church has conquered and will conquer still. By a love that is strong as death, she has always been victorious and must forever remain so. When she has not been ashamed to put the cross in the forefront, she has never had to be ashamed, for God has been with her, and Jesus has drawn all men to Himself. The crucified Christ has irresistible attractions. When He stoops into the utmost suffering and scorn, even the brutal must relent. A living Savior men may love, but a crucified Savior they must love. If they perceive that He loved them and gave Himself for them, their hearts are stolen away. The city of Mansoul is captured before the siege begins, when the Prince Emmanuel uncovers the beauties of His dying love before the eyes of the rebellious ones.*

# Chapter One

# The Marvelous Magnet

*"And I, if I be lifted up from the earth, will draw all men unto me. This he said, signifying what death he should die"*
—John 12:32–33.

JESUS IS THE SPOKESMAN here. He tells both of His own death by crucifixion and of the result that will follow. It appears, then, that our Lord's power to draw all men to Himself lies mainly in His death. By being lifted up from the earth upon the cross, He was made to die, and so also was He made to draw all men unto Himself. There is an attractive power about our Lord's person, and about His life, and about His teaching, but still the main attractive force lies in His death upon the cross. This is most certainly rare and strange, for when a great religious leader dies, a large measure of his personal power is gone. The charm of the man's manner, the impressiveness of his personal conviction, the lofty tone of his daily enthusiasm—these are immense helps to a cause while they are with us. To lose them is a fearful drawback that makes it perilous for a religious leader to die. Men may remember a leader's life for a time after his death, especially if he has been eminently good. But there is a limit to the influence of a mere memory. How often is it the case that after a little while, the leader having gone, the feebler folk gradually drop away, the hypocritical openly desert, the lukewarm wander, and so the cause dies out. The man's successors desert his principles or maintain them with but little life and energy, and therefore, what was once a hopeful effort expires like a burning candle. For a man's work to prosper, it is not desirable that he should die. Is it not strange that what is so often fatal to the influence of other men is a gain to our Lord Jesus Christ, for it is by His death that He possesses His most powerful influence over the sons of men? Because Jesus died, He is this day the mightiest ruler of human minds, the great center to which all hearts are being drawn.

Remember, too, that our Lord Jesus Christ died by a most shameful death. We have come to use the cross as an ornament, and by some it is regarded as an object of reverence. But the cross, to speak very plainly, was to the ancients what the gallows is to us—an odious instrument of death for felons—exactly that, and no more. The death of the cross was one never allotted to a Roman citizen except for certain heinous crimes. It was regarded as the death penalty of a slave. It was not only painful but also disgraceful and ignominious. To say that a man was crucified was in our Lord's time tantamount to saying today that he was hanged. It means just that; and you must accept the death of the cross with all the shame that can be connected with it, or else you will not understand what it meant to Jesus and His disciples. Now, surely, if a man is hanged, there is an end to his influence among men. When I was looking through all the Bible commentaries in the English language, I found one with a title page attributing it to Dr. Coke, but on further examination, I perceived that it was the commentary of Dr. Dodd, who was executed for forgery. After Dr. Dodd had been hanged, the publishers could not sell a commentary under his name, and so they engaged another scholar to take it under his wing. The man was hanged, and therefore people would not read his book, and you are not at all surprised that it should be so.

But herein is a wonderful thing. The Lord Jesus has lost no influence by having been hanged upon the tree. Rather, it is *because* of His shameful death that He is able to draw all men unto Himself. His glory rises from His humiliation; His adorable conquest from His ignominious death. When He "became obedient unto death, even the death of the cross" (Phil. 2:8), shame cast no shame upon His cause but gilded it with glory. Christ's death of weakness threw no weakness into Christianity, but rather it is the right arm of her power. By the sign of suffering unto death, the Church has conquered and will conquer still. By a love that is strong as death, she has always been victorious and must forever remain so. When she has not been ashamed to put the cross in the forefront, she has never had to be ashamed, for God has been with her, and Jesus has drawn all men to Himself. The crucified Christ has irresistible attractions. When He stoops into the utmost suffering and scorn, even the brutal must relent. A living Savior men *may* love, but a crucified Savior they *must* love. If they perceive that He loved them and gave Himself for them, their hearts are stolen away. The city of Mansoul is captured before the siege begins, when the Prince Emmanuel uncovers the beauties of His dying love before the eyes of the rebellious ones.)

Let us never be ashamed to preach Christ crucified—the Son of God lifted up to die among the condemned. Let those of us who teach in the Sunday school or preach at the street corner or in any other manner try to set forth the gospel always keep a dying Christ to the front. Christ without the cross is no Christ at all. Never forget that He is the eternal God, but bind with that truth the fact that He was nailed to a Roman cross. It is on the tree that He triumphed over Satan, and it is by the cross that He must triumph over the world. "I, if I be lifted up from the earth, will draw all men unto me. This he said, signifying what death he should die."

## The Attractive Force
## That Lies in a Crucified Savior

You will observe that it is briefly summed up in these words: *Himself* to *Himself.* "*I* will draw all men unto *me.*" It is not written that Christ will draw all men to the visible Church, for the universal profession of our holy faith is slow enough in coming. Certainly the Lord Jesus Christ will not lead Himself out to draw men to your denomination or to mine. (He will draw ever toward truth and righteousness but not to dead forms or meaningless distinctions,) nor to the memories of former wrongs or party victories. If the Lord should draw men to the cathedral or the tabernacle, the abbey or the chapel, it would be of little service to them unless in each case they found Him. The main thing that is wanted is that they be drawn to Him, and none can draw them to Him but He Himself. Himself drawing them to Himself—this is the soul of the text.

Perhaps you have heard the story of the missionaries among the Greenlanders. Our Moravian brethren, full of fire and zeal and self-denial, went among the ignorant folk of Greenland, longing to convert them. Using great prudence, they thought, "These people are in such darkness that it cannot be of any use to preach Jesus Christ to them at first. They do not even know that there is a God, so let us begin by teaching them the nature of the Deity, showing them right and wrong, proving to them the need of the atonement for sin, and setting before them the rewards of the righteous and the penalties of the wicked." This was judged to be a preparatory work. Watch for the result! They went on for years but had no converts. What was there in all that fine preparatory teaching that could convert anybody? Jesus was being locked out of the Greenlanders' heart by those who wanted Him to enter.

One day, one of the missionaries happened to read to a poor Greenlander the story of Jesus bleeding on the cross and how God had sent His Son to die, "that whosoever believeth in him should not perish, but have eternal life" (John 3:15). The Greenlander said, "Would you read me that again? What wonderful words! Did the Son of God die for us poor Greenlanders that we may live?" The missionary answered that it was so, and clapping his hands, the simple native cried, "Why did you not tell us that before?" Ah, just so! Why not tell them this at once and leave it to clear its own path? That is the point to begin with. Let us start with the Lamb of God that takes away the sin of the world. "For God so loved the world, that He gave His only begotten Son, that whosoever believeth in Him should not perish, but have everlasting life" (John 3:16). To my mind, that is the point to begin with and the point to go on with. Yes, that is the truth to conclude with, if there can ever be any conclusion to the grand old story of the incarnate God who loved His enemies and gave Himself to die in their stead, that they might live through Him. The gospel is Jesus drawing sinners to Himself that they might live through Him.

The text says that Jesus Christ will draw all men unto Himself. Now, all men who hear of Jesus Christ at all are drawn, but they do not all yield. Some of them pull back, and the most awful thing that ever happens to a man is when he pulls back till Jesus lets him go. What a fall is that, when the drawing power is taken away and the man falls backward into a destruction that he himself has chosen, having refused eternal life and resisted the Savior's power! Unhappy is the wretch who strives against his own salvation. Every man who hears the gospel feels some measure of its drawing power. I appeal to anyone who has been accustomed to hear it.

Does not Jesus sometimes tug hard at your conscience strings, and though you have pulled back, yet has He not drawn and drawn again? I remember how He drew *me* as a child, and, though I drew back from Him, yet did He never let me go till He drew me over the borderline. Some of you remember how you were drawn by a mother's gentle words, or by a teacher's earnest pleadings, or by a father's admonitions, or by a sister's tears, or by a pastor's entreaties. Permit your memories to aid me. Bring up before your mind's eye the many dear ones who have broken their hearts to win you for Jesus. Yes, you have been drawn.

I suppose that you have felt a measure of that drawing. It is not merely those who hear the gospel, but whole nations have been drawn, in other respects, by the all-pervading influence of Jesus and His love. At this instant, the influence of Christianity is being felt in every corner of the earth to an extent that it is not easy to exaggerate. If I had an orator's power, I would picture my Savior casting golden chains of love over all nations, wherever the missionary goes preaching His name. The Lord is taming the nations as a man by degrees subdues wild beasts. Jesus is gradually drawing the heathen to Himself. He has had a long tug at India. But it must come: it must yield. All those who watch it see that if there is any cause that does make progress in India, it is the cause of Christ. The East appears never to move, but if there is any move, it is Christward. Jesus is drawing China slowly. Japan is being drawn as in a net. Where the testimony of Christ has been borne, the idols begin to shake, and their priests confess that a change is coming. Every century sees a marked advance in the world's condition. And we shall progress at a quicker rate yet when the Church wakes up to a sense of her responsibility and the Holy Spirit is poured out upon the Church to turn us all into missionaries, causing us all in one way or another to preach the gospel of Christ.

Jesus is drawing, drawing, drawing. When God meant to scatter the individuals of our race, they would not be scattered. They built a tower to be the center of union, and only by their tongues being so changed that they could not understand one another could their resolve to remain in one company be defeated. But now, behold, the whole earth has the race of men to cover it, and it is the Father's will to gather together in one the redeemed of the Lord. Therefore He has set in their midst the great Shiloh, of whom it was prophesied of old, "Unto him shall the gathering of the people be"

(Gen. 49:10). The roaming races do not answer to the Father's call or want to come to the elder Brother's rule, but they will have to come, for He must reign. Gentile and Jew, African and European—they shall all meet at the cross, the common center of our entire manhood. For Christ is lifted up, and He is drawing all men unto Himself.

But not all men are saved. No, for when drawn, they do not come. Yet Christ crucified is drawing some men of all kinds and sorts to eternal life. When Jesus died on the cross, it was not for the nobility only, nor was it for the working man alone. It was for all sorts of people.

> *While grace is offered to the prince,*
> *The poor may take their share.*
> *No mortal has a just pretence*
> *To perish in despair.*

He who is best taught and instructed has often been drawn to Jesus by the Lord's overpowering charms. Some of the most educated of men have been delighted to come to Christ. But the most illiterate and rude have equally been drawn by Jesus, and it has been their joy to come. I love to hear of the gospel being preached to the poorest of the poor, and preached in a way that it reaches those who were never reached before. God speed every effort by which Jesus is set before the fallen and degraded, so long as it is the real gospel. Our fears begin only when Jesus is no longer in the message.

> *None are excluded hence but those*
> *Who do themselves exclude.*
> *Welcome the learned and polite,*
> *The ignorant and rude.*

There is no exclusion of any class or creature from the mercy of God in Christ Jesus. "I, if I be lifted up, will draw all men unto me." The history of the Church proves how true this is: the roll of the converted includes princes and paupers, masters and slaves.

But what is this force that attracts men to the crucified Savior? That they do come, there is no doubt about it. There is nothing in the world that men will hear so gladly as the gospel. How many years have I stood in my pulpit to preach to a great congregation.

The crowds have been here as regularly as the hours, Sunday after Sunday, morning and evening, year after year. Suppose that I had been appointed to preach upon a scientific subject. Could I have gained or held such audiences? I would have been tossed out a long while ago if I had been bound to draw upon myself for my matter. If I had preached any other than the doctrine of Christ crucified, I should years ago have scattered my audience to the winds of heaven. But the old theme is always new, always fresh, always attractive. Preach Jesus Christ. That is the recipe for catching men's ears and laying hold upon men's hearts. The name of Jesus is to man's heart that most mighty of charms. A man's ear waits for it as the morning hour waits for the sun or as the parched earth waits for the shower. Ring out the name of Jesus; it is the sweetest carol ever sung. Ring it out without fear or hesitation, for it is always welcome as the flowers in May. Men will never tire of it till the flowers are satiated with sunlight and the grass grows weary of the dew. The music of that blessed silver bell rings out o'er hill and dale as sweetly as when, on the first Christmas night, the angels sang, "Glory to God in the highest, and on earth peace, good will toward men" (Luke 2:14). There is about Calvary and its infinite stoop of divine love a power that never dies out and never will while the world stands. What is this universal attractiveness?

First, it is the force of *love,* for Jesus Christ is incarnate love. In Him you see one who divested Himself of all His glory, that He might save the guilty—who came down upon earth, not seeking wealth and fame but simply seeking to do good by saving men. He laid aside His honor and His glory, at last laid aside His life, and all for love, for love met a sad return. But it was a love that has saved its objects with a great salvation. Certainly, such love as the love of Christ, when it is told out simply and men can understand it, is certain to excite an interest, to win a degree of attention, and so to lead up to better things. Often this love proves its power over observers by transforming them from enemies into friends. Though they at first despised the Redeemer, His love compels them at length to believe and to adore. If I were asked the secret of the attractive power of the crucified Savior, I should answer that it is invincible love (The only crime that ever could be laid to Jesus' charge was that of loving beyond all reason and beyond all bound—loving as none ever loved before.) If all the rivers of human love did run together, they could not fill such another ocean of love as was in the heart of Jesus the Savior. This it is—the unique, unrivaled love—that draws men to Jesus. The pierced heart of Christ is a loadstone to draw all other hearts.

No doubt there is also this about the crucified Savior that He draws men: *the wonderful rest that His death provides for men.* The most earnest Christian man must sometimes have his doubts as to whether all is right with him. The more sincere a man is, the more does he tremble lest he should deceive himself. You may have your personal anxieties; certainly I have mine. But when I turn my eyes to Jesus upon the cross and view the thorn crown and the sacred head and the eyes that were red with weeping and the hands nailed fast to the wood and the feet dripping with blood, and when I remember that this shameful death was endured for love of me, I am so quiet and so happy in my spirit that I cannot tell how peacefully my life-floods flow. God *must* forgive my grievous fault, for my Redeemer has so grievously answered for it. When I see Jesus die, I perceive that henceforth divine justice is on the sinner's side. How can the Lord God punish the same offense twice—first the Substitute and then the men for whom that Substitute has bled? Christ has bled as substitute for every man who believes in Him—therefore is every believer safe.

O brethren, when you are troubled, rest with us by looking to Calvary. And if the first glance does not quiet you, look, and look, and look again, for every grief will die where Jesus died. Not to Bethlehem, where the stars of Christmas burn, do we look for our greatest comfort, but to that place where the sun was darkened at midday and the face of eternal love was veiled. Because the Lord of life and glory was dying *in extremis,* suffering the most deadly pain for our sakes, therefore His wounds distilled the richest balm that ever healed a sinner's wound. Men know this. Reading their Bibles, they soon find it out. There is no comfort for them against the anger of God and against their guilty consciences, until they see Christ in their place, suffering for them. The conscience sees with unspeakable delight the victim provided, and she gladly lays her hand on Jesus' head. She sees her sin transferred to Him, and punished in Him, and thus finds rest, like the rest of God. In the expiatory death of Jesus, the law is vindicated and God is "just, and the justifier of him which believeth" (Rom. 3:26).

Dear friend, believe me, Jesus bestows the peerless pearl of perfect rest on every heart that comes to Him. He fills the soul so that it has no more longings. You know the horseshoe magnet, and you have seen how rapidly it picks up pieces of iron. Have you ever put a piece of iron right across the two ends of the magnet? You will then have noticed that it ceases to attract anything else. The magnetic circuit is completed, and the magnet rests perfectly quiet, refusing to go beyond its own circle of pure content. When my soul is filled with Jesus, He completes the circuit of my soul's passions and longings. He is all my salvation and all my desire. Have you found it so? Has not your soul come to an absolutely perfect rest when it has gotten to Christ? When He Himself has drawn you to Himself, have you not entered into rest? Because men perceive that such a rest is to be had, they therefore come to Christ. He Himself uses this as an argument for why they should come. Remember His cheering words, ("Come unto me, all ye that labour and are heavy laden, and I will give you rest" (Matt. 11:28). This is part of the attractive force that dwells in a crucified Savior.)

Then, I am sure, there is a great attraction about Christ when we see *the change that He works in men.* Have you known a drunkard become a Christian or a thief become upright? Have you seen a harlot made chaste? Have you marked any of the modern miracles that are always going on around us in the form of conversions? If you have taken pleasure in these signs and wonders, I know that you have said, "Lord, I, too, will come to you to be converted." The sight of His power to elevate and sanctify has attracted you to Jesus, and you have fallen at His feet. There is no true, deep, tender living conversion except through the cross. Those who are taught of God do love to come to Christ, that sin may be conquered in them, that the heart of stone may be taken away, that the heart of flesh may be given, and that they may walk the happy way of holiness, according to the example of their adorable Master.

I could continue to show what this attractive force is, but lest I should weary you, I will only say that it lies much in *His sufferings themselves.* Is it not a strange thing that suffering attracts? Yes, lowly suffering conquers; she sits as a queen upon her throne and reigns by the royalty of her resignation. The ship of the Church has plowed her way through seas of blood; with the blood red cross at the masthead, she has pushed on even in the night, throwing the crimson spray about her. She has never paused because of persecution, affliction, or death—these are the rough winds that fill her sails. No progress is surer than that which comes of holy suffering.

The enemies of the Church have taken her disciples and burned them, but their deaths yielded a sweet savor of life. It is questionable whether a man's influence can be better promoted than by sending him aloft in a chariot of fire. What made England a Protestant nation for so many years? The stakes of Smithfield did it. Men and women stood and saw the martyrs burned, and as they saw them die, they said, "These men are right, and the cause for which they burn is true." Into the very heart of England, martyrdom cast up a way for the Lord Jesus, and He entered there and then into Old England's secret soul. What the martyrs did in their measure by their bitter death pangs is being done on a divine scale by the sufferings of the chief of all martyrs and head of all witnesses. By the agonies of Jesus, men's affections are moved and their hearts enthralled.

Are you unconverted but wish to be converted? I cannot suggest a better exercise than to read over the story of the death of Christ as it is told by the four evangelists. When you have read it once, read it again, and as you read it say, "Lord, I must have a sadly hard heart, or else this would move me to tears. I pray, change my heart." Then read the story again, for sure at last it will touch you. God the Holy Spirit blessing you, it will move you, and you will be among the "all men" that shall be drawn to Jesus by His own personal force.

## How Is This Force Exercised?

This force is exercised through the Holy Spirit. It is the Spirit of God who puts power into the truth about Christ, and then men feel that truth and come to Christ and live. But our blessed Lord and Master *uses instruments.* The force of Christ's love is sometimes shown to men by those who already love Him. One Christian makes many. One believer leads others to faith. To come back to my metaphor of a magnet, you have sometimes seen a battery attached to a coil. Then, if you take a nail and put it on the coil, the nail has become a strong magnet. You notice that the nail turns into a magnet, for you take another nail and put it on the end of it, and it holds the second nail fast. Now number two is turned into a magnet. Try it. Put a third nail upon it. See, it is held fast! Number three has become a magnet. And so it continues. On and on and on the magnetism goes, from one nail to another. But then go to your battery and detach one of your wires, and the nails drop off directly, for the coil has ceased to be a magnet, and the nails have ceased to be magnets, too. All the magnetism comes from the place from which it started, and when it ceases at the fountainhead, there is an end of it altogether. Indeed, Jesus Christ is the great attractive magnet, and all must begin and end with Him. When Jesus lays hold upon us, we get hold of a brother, and before long, he also turns into a magnet. Thus, from one to another the mystic influence proceeds, but the whole of the force abides in Jesus. More and more the kingdom grows, "ever mighty to prevail," but all the growing and the prevailing come out of Him. So it is that Jesus works—first by Himself and then by all who are in Him. May the Lord make us all magnets for Himself. Jesus says, "I, if I be lifted up, will draw all men unto me," but He leaves room in His figure for the co-working of all grateful hearts.

Jesus draws men *gradually*. Some are brought to Christ in a moment, but many are drawn by slow degrees. The sun in some parts of the world rises above the horizon in a single instant. But in our own country, at this season of the year, it is beautiful to watch the dawn, from the first gray light to the actual break of day. Is it dark or is it light? Well, it is not quite dark: it is darkness visible. By and by there is light. No sun is up as yet, but yet the light increases till the east begins to glow and the west reflects the radiance. Then, finally, up rises the great king of day. So does the Lord bring many to Himself by gentle degrees. They cannot tell when they were converted, but they are converted, for they have come to Christ. Rest assured that He will not send you back. Do not say, "I am not converted, for I do not know the moment of the great change." I knew an old lady once who did not know her birthday, but I never told her that she was not born because of that, for there she was. And if you do not know when you were made a Christian, yet, if you are Christian, it little matters when. If you are really born of God, the date of your new birth is interesting to curiosity but not important to godliness.

Salvation is often accomplished by a lengthened process. I have heard that when builders wanted to bridge a great chasm, they shot across the river an arrow or a bullet that drew with it a tiny thread. That was all the communication from bank to bank, and the rolling torrent was far below. Despise not the day of small things! The insignificant beginning was prophetic of grand results. By means of that little thread they drew across a piece of twine. When they had safely grasped it on the other side, they bound a small rope to the end of the twine, and they drew the rope across. Then to that rope they tied a cable, and they drew the cable across. And now over that chasm there strides an iron bridge, along which the train rattles with his mighty load. So does Jesus unite us to Himself. He may employ at first an insignificant thread of thought, then a sense of pleasant interest, then some deeper feeling, then a crushing emotion, then a faint faith, then stronger faith, then stronger yet, until, at last, we come to be firmly bound to Christ. Be thankful if you have only a thread of communication between you and Jesus, for it will lead to more. Something more hopeful will be drawn across the gulf before long. Christ's attractions are often very gradually revealed, and their victorious energy is not felt all at once.

Moreover, the cords of our Lord's drawings are very *secret*. You see the swallows twittering round our roofs, hawking in the air, shooting up into the clouds or flashing by our ear. It is summer, and they are paying us their annual visit. They will be with you for a time, and suddenly you will see them getting together about the gable of an old house, holding agitated congregations and evidently discussing matters of importance. The Lord of birds is gently drawing every swallow in England down toward the African coast, and they will all go, without exception, as the secret summons reaches the flying host. They know but little of the way, but their flight is not therefore delayed or its course left to uncertainty. Over thousands of miles of sea and land they pursue their course until they come to their resting place. And then, next spring, the same power that drew them south will draw them all north again, and hither they will come, and we shall hear their joyous twitter and say to ourselves, "Summer is coming, for here are the swallows again."

By a secret power of that order does Jesus draw home the strangers and the foreigners whom His grace has chosen. They say to one another, "Come, and let us go up to the house of the Lord. Let us seek the face of the Savior." The mystic attractions of the power of Christ are secretly drawing many who knew Him not, and now they ask their way to Zion with their face in its direction. Look how the sun draws along the planets. He hastens on in his mighty career space—I know not whither, but drawing with him all the worlds that compose the solar system. All these silently attend his majestic marches. Such is Christ, the great central sun; all His people follow, for He draws.

Fail not to observe *how gently* He does it! The classic heathens adored a goddess whom they represented as riding in a chariot drawn by doves. Surely the tenderest mode of impulse—power without force, motion born of emotion! Certain of us were drawn to Jesus by some such power. We could not but yield; the softness and tenderness of every touch of Jesus affected us infinitely more than force could possibly have done. Hearts are tender things and are not to be forced open with crowbars. The doors of the heart open gently to Him who holds the key, and who is that but He who made the heart and bought it with His precious blood? The gentleness is equal to the power when Jesus draws men to Himself!

But, oh, how *effectually!* I thought, as I considered this text, that I saw a great whirlpool like the maelstrom in the north of Norway. I thought I saw an enormous whirlpool so huge that all the souls of men, like ships of many forms, were being drawn toward it. With strained sight I gazed upon this monstrous death! Woe to those who are sucked in by that dreadful whirlpool, for there is no escape. The abyss has no bottom, destruction is sure to all who are caught in the tremendous down-rush! Even ships far out at sea on other tacks, though they escape this whirlpool, are hindered in their course by it, for this one monstrous devourer labors to absorb all and leaves no bay, nor harbor, nor foreign main unaffected by its perpetual draught. As I was thinking of this giant evil and wondering how I could navigate my own ship so as to avoid this mouth of hell, I saw a hand that had the mark of a nail upon its palm, and lo, it held a mighty magnet that attracted every vessel with a force greater than any born of sea or storm. This magnet attracted many ships so that they flew to it at once and were gently drawn toward their desired haven in the very teeth of the whirlpool. I saw other vessels in which the mariners hoisted sail to try to escape the influence of this magnet and even put out their oars to strive to get away; and some of them did so escape. Alas, they floated further and further into the whirlpool's destructive power, to be sucked down to their perdition. These were so besotted that they labored against mercy and resolved to be destroyed. I am glad that all are not left to act so madly.

You must have seen an instance of drawing very often down in the river. A grand vessel is bound for the ocean, but it is difficult to move the heavy craft. There it must lie. But here comes a tugboat. The large vessel hands a rope on board to the tug, and now the steam is up. Tug, tug, tug, and the big ship begins to follow the lead. It is no longer motionless; it will soon be walking the waters as a thing of life. A pleasant sight—the tug draws it gently out to sea and then leaves it to pursue its distant voyage. Just so may Jesus draw you away from sinful pleasures and from self-righteousness.

## What Does All This Imply?

It means that *men, by nature, are a long way off from Christ.* You were not born converted, of that I am sure. Nor were you born a Christian. And though they baptized you and said that they made you a "member of Christ, a child of God, and an inheritor of the kingdom of heaven," there was not a word of truth in it, for you loved sin and knew nothing of Christ. Unless God saves you, you will never get there. I may say of Christians who are made in that way, "Eyes have they, but they see not: They have ears, but they hear not:...neither speak they through their throat" (Ps. 115:5–7). And I fear that I must add, "They that make them are like unto them; so is every one that trusteth in them" (Ps. 115:8). It is a poor Christianity that is created by such monstrous folly. "Ye must be born again" (John 3:7), and you must be born again of the Spirit of God or you cannot enter the kingdom of heaven. Man is a long way off from Christ, and Christ must draw him. Friend, ask Him to draw *you.*

I gather also that *men will not come to Christ unless He draws them.* Sometimes, when I am trying to prepare a sermon to preach, I say to myself, "Why must I take all this trouble?" If men were in their senses, they would run to Christ without calling. Why must we put this business so temptingly? Why must we plead? Why must we be so earnest? Because men do not wish to be renewed in heart. They never will come—no, not one mother's son of them—unless He that sent Christ to them shall draw them to Christ. A work of grace in the heart is absolutely necessary before the sacrifice of the Lord Jesus will be accepted by any of us. Jesus said, "Ye will not come to me, that ye might have life" (John 5:40). What our Lord said is true to this hour; man has not improved an atom.

But, then, learn another lesson. If there is any man that Christ is drawing, he need not say, "May I come?" Of course, you may if you feel drawn to come. Are you coming? Come, and welcome. Christ never yet turned away a soul that came to Him—not one. "Him that cometh to me I will in no wise cast out" (John 6:37). If He is drawing you, run, for you have scriptural warrant for so doing. "Draw me, we will run after thee" (Song of Sol. 1:4). If you feel any kind of tugging at your heartstrings, do not stay a moment. Come along with you. When God draws, then is your time to move. What do the sailors say? "There's a breeze, Jack. Aye, aye, boys. Up with the anchor. Now for every stitch of canvas. We can make headway now." Do you feel any kind of breeze? Is the breath of the Holy Spirit moving upon you in any degree? Do you feel inclined to say, "I will go to Jesus"? Then, fly away with you, like a full-sailed ship before a fair wind. And by God's help, may you soon make the port of everlasting salvation.

Let us finish up by saying that if Christ has said that He will draw, then He will draw. The attractions of the Lord Jesus are continual. He draws, and He will always draw. He is drawing now. Do not pull back, lest His drawing should cease and you should perish. But rather let your heart sing:

> *He drew me, and I followed on,*
> *Charmed to confess the voice divine.*

O Spirit of God, draw men to Jesus. This is the way of salvation: Trust Christ, and you are saved. Rely wholly upon who Christ is and what He has done, and you are saved. In that very act there is a change effected within you that will show itself forever in your character, for he who believes in Jesus Christ, the Son of God, is born again. The faith that looks to Jesus and the life that lives upon that faith in Jesus come together. I cannot tell you which is first— the new birth or faith. Can you tell me which spoke of a wheel moves first? No. And these are spokes of one and the same wheel. "He that believeth on the Son hath everlasting life" (John 3:36). Oh believe Him! Trust Him! Lay hold upon Him! Accept Him, and go your way! And "the mountains and the hills shall break forth before you into singing, and all of the trees of the field shall clap their hands" (Isa. 55:12).

Amen. So let it be!

*Here is a picture of what we may expect from men if we are faithful to our Master. It is not likely that we shall be able to worship with their worship. They prefer a ceremonial pompous and gaudy; the swell of music, the glitter of costly garments, the parade of learning all these must minister grandeur to the world's religion and thus shut out the simple followers of the Lamb. The high places of earth's worship and honor are not for us. If we are true to our Master, we shall soon lose the friendship of the world. The sinful find our conversation distasteful. In our pursuits the carnal have no interest. Things dear to us are dross to worldlings, while things precious to them are contemptible to us. There have been times, and the days may come again, when faithfulness to Christ has entailed exclusion from what is called society. Even now to a large extent the true Christian is considered lower than the lowest caste in the judgment of some. The world has in former days counted it God's service to kill the saints. We are to reckon upon all this, and should the worst befall us, it is to be no strange thing to us. These are silken days, and religion fights not so stern a battle. I will not say it is because we are unfaithful to our Master that the world is more kind to us, but I half suspect it is, and it is very possible that if we were more thoroughly Christians, the world would more heartily detest us. If we would cleave more closely to Christ, we might expect to receive more slander, more abuse, less tolerance, and less favor from men.*

# Chapter Two

# The Procession of Sorrow

*And they took Jesus, and led him away*—John 19:16

IN THE DAYS TO COME, all eyes will be fixed on a great prince who shall ride through our London streets with his royal bride. I invite your attention to another Prince, marching in another fashion through His metropolis. London shall see the glory of the one: Jerusalem beheld the shame of the other. Come hither, ye lovers of Emmanuel, and I will show you this great sight—the King of sorrow marching to His throne of grief, the cross. I claim for the procession of my Lord an interest superior to the pageant Londoners are so anxiously expecting. Will the prince be sumptuously arrayed? Mine is adorned with garments crimsoned with His own blood. Will the prince be decorated with honors? Behold, my King is not without His crown—alas, a crown of thorns set with ruby drops of blood! Will the thoroughfares be thronged? So were the streets of Jerusalem, for great multitudes followed Him. Will they raise a clamor of tumultuous shouting? Such a greeting had the Lord of glory, but alas, it was not the shout of welcome but the yell of "Away with him, away with him" (John 19:15). High in the air they bid their banners wave about the heir of England's throne, but how shall you rival the banner of the sacred cross that day for the first time borne among the sons of men. For the thousands of eyes that shall gaze upon the youthful prince, I offer the gaze of men and angels. All nations gathered about my Lord, both great and mean men clustered around His person. From the sky the angels viewed Him with wonder and amazement. The spirits of the just looked from the windows of heaven upon the scene; yea, the great God and Father watched each movement of His suffering Son.

Oh, I pray you, lend your ears to such faint words as I can write on a subject all too high for me, the march of the world's Maker along the way of His great sorrow! Your Redeemer traverses the rugged path of suffering, along which He went with heaving heart and heavy footsteps, that He might pave a royal road of mercy for His enemies.

## Christ As Led Forth

Pilate scourged our Savior according to the common custom of Roman courts. The lictors executed their cruel office upon His shoulders with their rods and scourges until the stripes had reached the full number. Jesus is formally condemned to crucifixion, but before He is led away He is given over to the Praetorian guards so that those rough Roman legionaries may insult Him. It is said that a German regiment was at that time stationed in Judea, and I should not wonder whether they were the lineal ancestors of those German theologians of modern times who have mocked the Savior, tampered with revelation, and cast the vile spittle of their philosophy into the face of truth. The soldiers mocked and insulted Him in every way that cruelty and scorn could devise. The platted crown of thorns, the purple robe, the reed with which they smote Him, and the spittle with which they disfigured Him, all these marked the contempt in which they held the King of the Jews. The reed was no mere rush from the brook. It was of a stouter kind used for walking staves, and the blows were cruel as well as insulting. The crown was not of straw but of thorn; hence, it produced pain as well as pictured scorn. When they had mocked Him, they pulled off the purple garment He had worn, causing much pain. His wounds unstaunched and raw, fresh bleeding from beneath the lash, would make this scarlet robe adhere to Him, and when it was dragged off, His gashes would bleed anew.

We do not read that they removed the crown of thorns, and therefore it is most probable, though not absolutely certain, that our Savior wore it along the Via Dolorosa and bore it upon His head when He was fastened to the cross. The pictures that represent our Lord as wearing the crown of thorns upon the tree have therefore at least *some* scriptural warrant: They put His own clothes upon Him because they were part of the payment of the executioner. As modern hangmen take the garments of those whom they execute, so did the four soldiers claim a right to His raiment. They put on Him His own clothes that the multitude might discern Him to be the same man, the very man who had professed to be the Messiah. We all know that different clothing will often raise a doubt about the identity of an individual. But the people saw Him in the street, not arrayed in the purple robe but wearing His garment without seam, woven from the top throughout, the common smock frock of the countrymen of Palestine, and they said at once, "Yes, 'tis He, the man who healed the sick, and raised the dead; the mighty teacher who sat upon the mountaintop or stood in the temple courts and preached with authority, and not as the scribes." There can be no shadow of doubt but that our Lord was really crucified, and no one substituted for Him.

How they led Him forth we do not know. Some expositors tell us that He had a rope about His neck with which they roughly dragged Him to the tree. We care, however, far more for the fact that He went forth carrying His cross upon His shoulders. This was intended at once to proclaim His guilt and intimate His doom. Usually the crier went before with an announcement such as this: "This is Jesus of Nazareth, King of the Jews, who for making Himself a king and stirring up the people, has been condemned to die." This cross was not so heavy, perhaps, as some pictures would represent it, but still was no light burden to a man whose shoulders were raw with the lashes of the Roman scourge. Jesus had been all night in agony. He had spent the early morning at the hall of Caiaphas. He had been hurried from Caiaphas to Pilate, from Pilate to Herod, from Herod back again to Pilate. He had, therefore, but little strength left, and you will not wonder that by and by we find Him staggering beneath His load and that another is called to bear it with Him. He goes forth, then, bearing His cross.

What do we learn as we see Christ led forth? Do we not see here the truth of that which was set forth in shadow by *the scapegoat*? Did not the high priest bring the scapegoat and put both his hands upon its head, confessing the sins of the people, that those sins might be laid upon the goat? Then the goat was led away into the wilderness, and it carried away the sins of the people, so that if they were sought for, they could not be found. Now we see Jesus brought before the priests and rulers, who pronounce Him guilty. God Himself imputes our sins *to Him*. He was made sin for us, and as the substitute for our guilt, bearing our sin upon His shoulders—for that cross was a sort of representation in wood of our guilt and doom—we see the great Scapegoat led away by the appointed officers of justice. Bearing upon His back the sin of all His people, the offering goes without the camp. Beloved, can you say He carried *your* sin? As you look at the cross upon His shoulder does it represent *your* sin? Oh, raise the question, and be not satisfied unless you can answer it most positively in the affirmative! There is one way by which you can tell whether He carried your sin or not. Have you laid your hand upon His head, confessed your sin, and trusted in Him? Then your sin lies not on you. Not one single ounce of it lies on you. It has all been transferred by blessed imputation to Christ, and He bears it on His shoulder in the form of yonder heavy cross. What joy, what satisfaction this will give if we can sing:

> *My soul looks back to see*
> *The burden Thou didst bear,*
> *When hastening to the accursed tree,*
> *And knows her guilt was there!*

Do not let the picture vanish till you have satisfied yourself once for all that Christ was here the substitute for you.

Let us muse upon the fact that Jesus was conducted without the gates of the city. It was *the common place of death*. That little rising ground, which perhaps was called Golgotha, the place of a skull from its somewhat resembling the crown of a man's skull, was a common place of execution. It was one of Death's castles. Here he stored his gloomiest trophies and was the grim lord of that stronghold. Our great hero, the Destroyer of Death, bearded the lion in his den, slew the monster in his own castle, and dragged the dragon captive from his own den. I think Death thought it a splendid triumph when he saw the Master impaled and bleeding in the dominions of destruction. Little did he know that the grave was to be rifled and himself destroyed by that crucified Son of Man.

Was not the Redeemer led here *to aggravate His shame?* Calvary was the usual place of execution for the district. Christ must die a felon's death, and it must be upon the felon's gallows, in the place where horrid crimes had met their due reward. This added to His shame; but I think in this, too, He draws the nearer to us. "He was numbered with the transgressors; and he bare the sin of many, and made intercession for the transgressors" (Isa. 53:12).

But further, this is the great lesson from Christ's being slaughtered without the gate of the city—*let us go forth, therefore, without the camp, bearing His reproach.* You see there the multitude *are leading Him forth from the temple.* He is not allowed to worship with them. The ceremonial of the Jewish religion denies Him any participation in its pomp. The priests condemn Him never again to tread the hallowed floors, never again to look upon the consecrated altars in the place of His people's worship. He is exiled from *their friendship,* too. No man dare call Him friend now or whisper a word of comfort to Him. He is banished from their *society,* as if he were a leper whose breath would be infectious, whose presence would scatter plague. They force Him without the walls and are not satisfied till they have rid themselves of his obnoxious presence. For Him they have no tolerance. Barabbas may go free. The thief and the murderer may be spared. But for Christ there is no word, but "Away with such a fellow from the earth! It is not fit that He should live." Jesus is therefore hunted out of the city, beyond the gate, with the will and force of His own nation, but He journeys not against His own will. Even as the lamb goes as willingly to the altar as to the meadow, so does Christ cheerfully take up His cross and go without the camp.

Here is a picture of what we may expect from men if we are faithful to our Master. It is not likely that we shall be able to worship with their worship. They prefer a ceremonial pompous and gaudy; the swell of music, the glitter of costly garments, the parade of learning all these must minister grandeur to the world's religion and thus shut out the simple followers of the Lamb. The high places of earth's worship and honor are not for us. If we are true to our Master, we shall soon lose the friendship of the world. The sinful find our conversation distasteful. In our pursuits the carnal have no interest. Things dear to us are dross to worldlings, while things precious to them are contemptible to us. There have been times, and the days may come again, when faithfulness to Christ has entailed exclusion from what is called *society*. Even now to a large extent the true Christian is considered lower than the lowest caste in the judgment of some. The world has in former days counted it God's service to kill the saints. We are to reckon upon all this, and should the worst befall us, it is to be no strange thing to us. These are silken days, and religion fights not so stern a battle. I will not say it is because we are unfaithful to our Master that the world is more kind to us, but I half suspect it is, and it is very possible that if we were more thoroughly Christians, the world would more heartily detest us. If we would cleave more closely to Christ, we might expect to receive more slander, more abuse, less tolerance, and less favor from men.

You young believers, who have lately followed Christ, should father and mother forsake you, remember you were bidden to reckon upon it; should brothers and sisters deride you, you must put this down as part of the cost of being a Christian. Godly workingmen, should your employers or your fellow workers frown upon you; wives, should your husbands threaten to cast you out, remember, without the camp was Jesus' place and without the camp is yours. Oh, you Christian men, who dream of trimming your sails to the wind, who seek to win the world's favor, I do beseech you to cease from a course so perilous! We are in the world, but we must never be of it. We are not to be secluded like monks in the cloister, but we are to be separated like Jews among Gentiles. We are to be men, but not of men; helping, aiding, befriending, teaching, comforting, instructing, but not sinning, either to escape a frown or to win a smile. The more manifestly there shall be a great gulf between the Church and the world, the better shall it be for both. It is better for the world, for it shall be thereby warned. It is better for the Church, for it shall be thereby preserved. Go, then, like the Master, expecting to be abused, to wear an ill name, and to earn reproach. Go, like Him, without the camp.

## Christ Carrying His Cross

I have shown you, believer, your position; let me now show you your *service*. Christ comes forth from Pilate's hall with the cumbersome wood upon His shoulder, but through weariness He travels slowly. His enemies, half afraid from His emaciated appearance that He may die before He reaches the place of execution, allow another to carry His burden. The tender mercies of the wicked are cruel; they cannot spare Him the agonies of dying on the cross, but they will therefore remit the labor of carrying it. They place the cross upon Simon, a Cyrenian, coming out of the country. Simon was an African, for he came from Cyrene. We are not sure that Simon was a disciple of Christ. He may have been a friendly spectator, yet one would think the Jews would naturally select a disciple if they could. Coming fresh from the country, not knowing what was going on, Simon joined with the mob, and they made him carry the cross. Whether a disciple then or not, we have every reason to believe that he became so afterward. He was the father, we read, of Alexander and Rufus, two persons who appear to have been well-known in the early Church. Let us hope that salvation came to his house when he was compelled to bear the Savior's cross.

Dear friend, remember that although no one died on the cross with Christ—for atonement must be executed by a solitary Savior—yet another person did carry the cross for Christ. This world, while redeemed by price by Christ and by Christ alone, is to be redeemed by divine power manifested in the sufferings and labors of the saints as well as those of Christ. Mark you, the *ransom* of men was all paid by Christ; that was redemption *by price*. But power is wanted to dash down those idols, to overcome the hosts of error. Where is it to be found? In the Lord of Hosts who shows His power in the sufferings of Christ and of His Church. The Church must suffer, that the gospel may be spread by her means. This is what the apostle meant when he said, "[I] fill up that which is behind of the afflictions of Christ in my flesh for his body's sake, which is the church" (Col. 1:24). There was nothing behind in the price, but there is something behind in the manifested power. We must continue to fill up that measure of revealed power, carrying the cross with Christ until the last shame shall have been poured upon His cause and He shall reign forever and ever. We see in Simon's carrying the cross a picture of what the Church is to do throughout all generations. Mark then, Christian, Jesus does not suffer so as to exclude your suffering. He bears a cross, not that you may escape it but that you may endure it. Christ does exempt you from sin but not from sorrow. He does take the curse of the cross, but He does not take the cross of the curse away from you. Remember that and expect to suffer.

Beloved, let us comfort ourselves with this thought, that in our case, as in Simon's, *it is not your cross, but Christ's cross that we carry.*

When you are treated badly for your godliness, when your religion brings the trial of cruel mockings upon you, then remember, it is not *your* cross, it is *Christ's* cross. How delightful is it to carry the cross of our Lord Jesus?

*You carry the cross after Him.* You have blessed company. Your path is marked with footprints of your Lord. If you will look, there is the mark of His blood red shoulder upon that heavy cross. 'Tis *His* cross, and He goes before you as a shepherd goes before his sheep. Take up your cross daily and follow Him.

Do not forget, also, *that you bear this cross in partnership.* It is the opinion of some commentators that Simon carried only one end of the cross and not the whole of it. That is very possible. Christ may have carried the heavier end, against the transverse beam, and Simon may have borne the lighter end. Certainly it is so with you. You do but carry the lighter end of the cross; Christ bore the heavier end.

> *His way was much rougher and darker than mine;*
> *Did Christ, my Lord, suffer, and shall I repine?*

Rutherford says, "Whenever Christ gives us a cross, He cries, 'Halves, my love.'" Others think that Simon carried the whole of the cross. If he carried all the cross, yet he carried only the wood of it, he did not bear the sin that made it such a load. Christ did but transfer to Simon the outward frame, the mere tree. But the curse of the tree, which was our sin and its punishment, rested on Jesus' shoulders still. Dear friend, if you think that you suffer all that a Christian can suffer, if all God's billows roll over you, yet remember, there is not one drop of wrath in all your sea of sorrow. Jesus took the wrath. Jesus carried the sin. Now all that you endure is but for His sake, that you may be conformed in His image and may aid in gathering His people into His family.

Although Simon carried Christ's cross, *he did not volunteer to do it, but they compelled him.* Beloved, I fear that most of us, if we ever do carry it, carry it by compulsion. At least when it first comes onto our shoulders, we do not like it and would run from it, but the world compels us to bear Christ's cross. Cheerfully accept this burden, you servants of the Lord. I do not think we should seek after needless persecution. That man is a fool and deserves no pity who purposely excites the disgust of other people. No, we must not make a cross of our own. Let there be nothing but religion to object to, and then if that offends them, let them be offended; it is a cross that you must carry joyfully.

*Though Simon had to bear the cross for a very little while, it gave him lasting honor.* I do not know how far it was from Pilate's house to the Mount of Doom. The city of Jerusalem has been so razed and burned that there is little chance of distinguishing any of these positions, with the exception, it may be, of Mount Calvary, which being outside the walls may possibly still remain. The Via Dolorosa is a long street at the present time, but then it may have been but a few yards. Simon has to carry the cross but for a very little time, yet his name is in this Book forever, and we may envy him his honor. Well, beloved, the cross we have to carry is only for a little while at most. A few times the sun will go up and down the hill, a few more moons will wax and wane, and then we shall receive the glory. "For our light affliction, which is but for a moment, worketh for us a far more exceeding and eternal weight of glory" (2 Cor. 4:17).

We should love the cross and count it very dear because it works out for us a far more exceeding and eternal weight of glory. Christians, will you refuse to be cross bearers for Christ? I am ashamed of some professing Christians—heartily ashamed of them! Some of them have no objection to worship with a poor congregation until they grow rich, and then they must go with the world's church to mingle with fashion and gentility. There are some who in certain company hold their tongues and never say a good word for Christ. They take matters very gently. They think it unnecessary to be soldiers of the cross. "He that taketh not his cross, and followeth after me," says Christ, "is not worthy of me" (Matt. 10:38). Some will not be baptized because they think people will say, "He is a professor; how holy he should be." I am glad the world expects much from us and watches us closely. All this is a blessed means of keeping us nearer the Lord. Oh, you who are ashamed of Christ, how can you read that text! "For whosoever shall be ashamed of me and of my words, of him shall the Son of man be ashamed, when he shall come in his own glory, and in his Father's, and of the holy angels" (Luke 9:26). Conceal your religion? Cover it with a cloak? God forbid! Our religion is our glory. The cross of Christ is our honor, and while not ostentatiously parading it, as the Pharisees do, we should never be so cowardly as to conceal it. Take up your cross and go without the camp, following your Lord, even until death.

## Christ and His Mourners

As Christ went through the streets, a great multitude looked on. In the multitude there was a sparse sprinkling of tender-hearted women, probably those who had been blessed by Him. Some of these were persons of considerable rank, many of them had ministered to Him of their substance. Amidst the din and howling of the crowd, they raised an exceeding loud and bitter cry, like Rachel weeping for her children, who would not be comforted. The voice of sympathy prevailed over the voice of scorn. Jesus paused and said, "Daughters of Jerusalem, weep not for me, but weep for yourselves, and for your children" (Luke 23:28). The sorrow of these good women was a very proper sorrow. Jesus did not by any means forbid it, He only recommended another sorrow as being better. If we weep for the sufferings of Christ in the same way as we lament the sufferings of another man, our emotions will be only natural and may work no good. They would be very proper, and God forbid that we should stay them, except with the gentle words of Christ, "Daughters of Jerusalem, weep not for me." The most scriptural way to describe the sufferings of Christ is not by laboring to excite sympathy through highly colored descriptions of His blood and wounds. Some have played upon the feelings of the people in this manner, and to a degree the attempt is commendable, but if it shall all end in tears of pity no good is done. I have heard sermons and studied works upon the passion and agony that have moved me to copious tears, but I am not sure that all the emotion was profitable. I show you a more excellent way.

What, then, dear friends, should be the sorrows excited by a view of Christ's sufferings? They are these: *Weep not because the Savior bled, but because your sins made Him bleed.*

> 'Twere you my sins, my cruel sins,
> His chief tormentors were;
> Each of my crimes became a nail,
> And unbelief the spear.

When a brother makes confession of his transgressions before God, he humbles himself with many tears. I am sure the Lord thinks far more of the tears of repentance than He would do of the mere drops of human sympathy. "Weep for yourselves," says Christ, "rather than for me."

The sufferings of Christ *should make us weep over those who have brought that blood upon their heads.* We ought not to forget the Jews. Those once highly favored people of God who cursed themselves with, "His blood be on us, and on our children" (Matt. 27:25), should make us mourn when we think of their present degradation. There are no passages in all the public ministry of Jesus so tender as those that regard Jerusalem. It is sorrow not over Rome but over Jerusalem. I believe there was a tenderness in Christ's heart to the Jew of a special character. Jesus loved the Gentile, but still Jerusalem was the city of the Great King. It was, "O Jerusalem, Jerusalem,…how often would I have gathered thy children together, as a hen doth gather her brood under her wings, but ye would not!" (Luke 13:34). Christ saw its streets flowing like bloody rivers. He saw the temple flaming up to heaven. He marked the walls loaded with Jewish captives crucified by command of Titus. He saw the city razed to the ground and sown with salt, and He said, "Weep not for me, but weep for yourselves, and for your children. For, behold, the days are coming,…Then shall they begin to say to the mountains, Fall on us; and to the hill, Cover us" (Luke 23:28–30).

Let me add that when we look at the sufferings of Christ, *we ought to sorrow deeply for the souls of all unregenerate men and women.* Remember that what Christ suffered for us, these unregenerate ones must suffer for themselves unless they put their trust in Christ. The woes that broke the Savior's heart must crush theirs. Either Christ must die for me, or else I must die for myself the second death. If He did not carry the curse for me, then on me must it rest forever and ever. Think, dear friend, there are some who as yet have no interest in Jesus' blood, some sitting next to you, your nearest friends who, if they were now to close their eyes in death, would open them in hell! Think of that! Weep not for Him, but for these. Perhaps they are your children, the objects of your fondest love, with no interest in Christ, without hope in the world! Save your tears for them. Christ asks them not in sympathy for Himself. Think of the millions in this dark world! When we know how very small a proportion of the human race have even nominally received the cross—and there is no other name given under heaven among men whereby we must be saved (Acts 4:12)—oh, what a black thought crosses our mind! What a cataract of immortal souls dashes downward to the pit every hour! Well might the Master say, "Weep not for me, but for yourselves." You have, then, no true sympathy for Christ if you have not an earnest sympathy with those who would win souls for Christ. You may sit under a sermon and feel a great deal, but your feeling is worthless unless it leads you to weep for yourself and for your children. How has it been with you? Have you repented of sin? Have you prayed for your fellow men? If not, may that picture of Christ fainting in the streets lead you to do so now.

## Christ's Fellow Sufferers

There were two other cross bearers in the throng who were malefactors. Their crosses were just as heavy as the Lord's, and yet one of them had no sympathy with Him, and his bearing the cross only led to his death and not to his salvation. I have sometimes met with persons who have suffered much, have worked hard all of their lives, or have laid for years upon a bed of sickness, and they therefore suppose that because they have suffered so much in this life, they shall thus escape the punishment of sin hereafter. I tell you that yonder malefactor carried his cross and died on it, and you will carry your sorrow and be damned with them unless you repent. That impenitent thief went from the cross of his great agony—and it was agony indeed to die on a cross—to that place, to the flames of hell. You, too, may go from the bed of sickness and from the abode of poverty to perdition quite as readily as from the home of ease and the house of plenty. No sufferings of ours have anything to do with the atonement of sin. No blood but that which *He* has spilt, no groans but those that came from *His* heart, no suffering but that which was endured by *Him*, can ever make a recompense for sin. Shake off the thought, any of you who suppose that God will have pity on you because you have endured affliction. You must consider Jesus and not yourself. Turn your eye to Christ, the great Substitute for sinners, but never dream of trusting in yourself.

## The Savior's Warning Question

*"If they do these things in the green tree, what will they do in the dry?"* Among other things, I think He meant this: "If I, the innocent Substitute for sinners, suffer thus, what will be done when the sinner himself—the dry tree—whose sins are his own and not merely imputed to him, shall fall into the hands of an angry God?" Remember that when God saw Christ in the sinner's place, He did not spare Him, and when He finds you without Christ, He will not

spare *you*. You have seen Jesus led away by His enemies; so shall you be dragged away by fiends to the place appointed for you. It shall be fulfilled to you: "Depart from me, ye cursed, into everlasting fire, prepared for the devil and his angels" (Matt. 25:41). Jesus was deserted of God and if He, who was only imputedly a sinner, was deserted, how much more shall you be? *"Eloi, Eloi, lama sabachthani"*—what an awful shriek! But what shall be your cry when you shall say, "Good God! Why hast thou forsaken me?" and the answer shall come back, "Because I have called, and ye refused; I have stretched out my hand, and no man regarded; but ye have set at nought all my counsel, and would none of my reproof: I also will laugh at your calamity; I will mock when your fear cometh" (Prov. 1:24–26). These are awful words, but they are not mine. They are the very words of God in Scripture. If God hides His face from Christ, how much less will He spare you! He did not spare His Son the stripes. What whips of steel for you, what knots of burning wire for you, when conscience shall smite you, when the law shall scourge you with its ten-thonged whip! Oh, who would stand in your place when God shall say, "Awake, O sword, against the rebel, against the man who rejected me; smite him, and let him feel the smart forever!" Christ was spit upon with shame; what shame will be yours! The whole universe shall hiss you. Angels shall be ashamed of you. Your own friends, yes, your sainted mother, shall say "Amen" to your condemnation. And those who loved you best shall sit as assessors with Christ to judge you and condemn you! I cannot roll up into one word all the mass of sorrows that met upon the head of Christ who died for us; therefore, it is impossible for me to tell you what streams, what oceans of grief, must roll over *your* spirit if you die as you now are. You may die so, and you may die now. I do beseech you, by the agonies of Christ, by His wounds and by His blood, do not bring upon yourself the curse. Do not bear in your own person the awful wrath to come! May God deliver you! Trust in the Son of God and you shall never die.

*That* was a dreadful spectacle that I pictured to you just now—our Lord bearing His cross and the women weeping. But how much more awful is that before me! I see a soul carrying about itself the instrument of its own destruction and going onward to its doom! Sin is the cross to which the soul will be fastened, and habits and depravities are the nails. The soul is bearing its sin and loving to bear it. See, it is going to execution, but at each step it laughs. Every step it takes is bearing it toward hell, and yet it makes mirth! Lo, the infatuated one scoffs at the voice that warns him, and every scoff he utters is increasing his guilt. Look forward to his end, its never-ending end. Look forward to it steadily, with calm and tearful gaze. Is it not an awful spectacle? But what if you should be beholding yourself as in a vision or seeing your child in the glass of prophecy! If it be your case, I beseech you repent of your sin, bewail your condition, and fly to Christ for shelter. And if it is your child, give heaven no rest, plead continually at the throne of grace till you have brought down a blessing from God upon your offspring. Never cease to pray until your sons and your daughters are safe landed on the Rock of Ages and so secured there they will need no other rock to hide them in the day when Christ shall come. I beseech you, ask for tenderness toward sinners, toward all sinners, and let your tenderness be shown in fervent prayer, in incessant effort, and in holy sympathy toward the wandering ones.

# Chapter Three

# Wherefore Should I Weep?

*And there followed him a great company of people, and of women, which also bewailed and lamented him. But Jesus turning unto them said, Daughters of Jerusalem, weep not for me, but weep for yourselves, and for your children. For, behold, the days are coming, in the which they shall say, Blessed are the barren, and the wombs that never bare, and the paps which never gave suck. Then shall they begin to say to the mountains, Fall on us; and to the hills, Cover us. For if they do these things in a green tree, what shall be done in the dry? —Luke 23:27–31.*

CAN YOU PICTURE THE SCENE? Jesus is given up by Pilate to the Jews that they may do their will with Him, and led by a small band of soldiers, He is conducted into the public street, bearing His cross upon His shoulders. Perhaps they judged Him to be weary with His night of watching and worn with His sufferings from the scourge, and they feared lest He might die upon the road. Therefore, with a cruel mercy they laid hold upon someone in the crowd who had too loudly expressed his sympathy, forced him into military service, and compelled him to assist in carrying the instrument of execution. You see the haughty scribes and the ribald throng; but the center of the spectacle, and the cause of it all was our Lord Himself, Jesus of Nazareth, the King of the Jews.

We cannot paint Him; all who have ever attempted to do so have to a large extent been unsuccessful, for there was upon His face a mingled majesty and meekness, loveliness and lowliness, sanctity and sorrow, that it would not be possible to express upon canvas or to represent in words. About His person were abundant marks of cruelty. He had been scourged; everyone could see it. His own garments that they had put upon Him could not conceal the marks of the Roman lash. The traces of the crown of thorns were on His brow, and the rough treatment of the soldiers had left its tokens, too, so that His face was more marred than that of any man, and His form more than the sons of men. And now He is being led away to be put to the shameful death of the cross.

There were some glad eyes there, delighted that at last their victim was in their power and that the eloquent tongue that had exposed their hypocrisy would now be silenced in death. There, too, were the unfeeling Romans, to whom human life was a trifle, and all around gathered in dense masses the brutal mob, bribed to shout against their best Friend. But all then present were not in this savage mood. There were some—and to the honor of the gender it is recorded that they were women—who entered their protest by their cries and lamentations. Not silently in their sorrow did they weep, but they began to lament aloud and bewail audibly, as though they were attending the funeral of some dear friend or expected the death of one of their kindred. The voice of a woman's weeping has great power with most of us, but it would not stir the stony hearts of Roman legionaries. The wail of women was no more to the solders than the moaning of the winds among the forest trees. Yet it must have struck many of less stern and uncaring men and filled their souls with some measure of kindred feeling. Chiefly, however, did it strike One, the tenderest hearted among them all, One whose ear was delicately sensitive to every sound of sorrow. And though Jesus had not answered Herod and had given Pilate but a few words of reply, and amidst all the mockeries and scourgings He had been as dumb as a sheep before her shearers, yet He paused, and looking round upon the weeping company, piteously yet sublimely broke the silence by saying to them, "Weep not for me, but weep for yourselves, and for your children." Such was the scene.

As for the words themselves, they are especially noteworthy because they constitute the last connected discourse of the Savior before He died. All that He said afterward was fragmentary and mainly of the nature of prayer. A sentence to John, and to His own

mother, and to the dying thief: just a word or two looking downward, but for the most part He uttered broken sentences that flew
upward on the wings of strong desire. This was His last address, a
farewell sermonette, and it was delivered amid surroundings most
sad and solemn, restraining tears and yet at the same time causing
them to flow. We consider the words to be all the more weighty and
full of solemnity because of the occasion, but even apart from this,
the truths delivered were in themselves of the utmost importance.
This last discourse of our Lord before His death was terribly
prophetic to a world rejecting Him, portentous with a thousand
woes to a people whom He loved, woes that even He could not
avert because they had rejected His reconciliation and refused the
mercy that He came to bring. "Daughters of Jerusalem," said He,
"weep not for me, but weep for yourselves, and for your children."
Not many hours before He had Himself set them the example by
weeping over the doomed city, and crying, "O Jerusalem,
Jerusalem, thou that killest the prophets, and stonest them which
are sent unto thee, how often would I have gathered thy children
together, even as a hen gathereth her chickens under her wings,
and ye would not!" (Matt. 23:37).

Looking even upon the surface of the words, you will perceive
that they bear His undoubted image and superscription. Who but
He would have spoken like this? You are sure that the passage is
genuine, for it is in all respects so inimitably Christlike. See how
selfless He was, for Himself He asks not even tears of sympathy.
Was there no cause for grief? Yes, cause enough. Yet He says,
"Weep not for me, but weep for yourselves," as if all His thoughts
were taken up with other griefs than His own, and He would not
have a tear wasted upon Him, but spent on woes that grieved Him
more than His own pangs. Observe the majesty of the speech, too,
steeped as the speaker was in misery. You can see that His is sorrow that is well deserved to be wept over, but He is not overcome
by it. Rather His royal soul reigns in the future, and as a King He
anticipates His scepter and His judgment seat, foretelling the doom
of those who now insult Him.

Here is no cowardly spirit, no confession of defeat, no appeal
for pity, no shadow of petty resentment, but on the contrary a
majestic consciousness of strength. With His calm, prophetic eye
He looks beyond the intervening years and sees Jerusalem
besieged and captured. He speaks as though He heard the awful

shrieks that sound the entrance of the Romans into the city and the smiting down of young and old, women and children. Behold how His piercing eye sees further yet: He describes the day when He shall sit upon the throne of judgment and summon all men to His bar, when He who was then the weary Man before His foes should alarm the ungodly by the appearance of His countenance, so that they would call to the mountains to fall upon them and to the hills to hide them from His face. He speaks as if conscious of the majesty that would be upon Him in that dreadful day, and yet at the same time pitiful toward those who by their sins were bringing upon themselves so terrible a doom. He says, in effect, "Weep for those concerning whom it would have been better that they had never been born and for whom annihilation would be a consummation deeply to be desired." He dries up the tears that were flowing for Him, that the women may draw upon the reservoirs of their souls and let the torrents of their grief flow forth for impenitent sinners who will be filled with unutterable dismay at His second coming.

## Weep Not

He said to the weeping women, "Weep not." There are some cold, calculating expositors who say that our Lord reproved these women for weeping and that there was something wrong or, if not altogether wrong, yet something very far from commendable in their sorrow—I think they call it "the sentimental sympathy" of these kind souls. There is no human much more unnatural than a cold-blooded commentator who bites at every letter and nibbles at the grammatical meaning of every syllable, translating with his lexicon but never exercising common sense or allowing even the least play to his heart. Blame these women! No, *bless* them again and again. It was the one redeeming trait in the dread march along the Via Dolorosa. Let it not be dreamed that Jesus could have censured those who wept for Him. No, no, no, a thousand times no! These gentle women appear in a happy contrast to the chief priests with their savage malice and to the thoughtless multitude with their fierce cry of "Crucify him, crucify him." They seem to me to have shown a noble courage in daring to express their sympathy with one whom everybody else hunted to death with such ferocity. To espouse His cause amid those hoarse cries of "Crucify him, crucify him," was courage more than manly; those women were heroines more valiant than those who rush upon the spoil. Those lamentations in sympathy with Him who was being led to die are worthy of our praise and not of our criticism. Our Lord accepted the sympathy they evinced, and it was only His great disinterested unselfishness that made Him say, "Spare your griefs for other sorrows." It was not because they were wrong but because there was something still more necessary to be done than even to weep for Him.

There can be nothing wrong with the weeping of these women; therefore, let us proceed to say, first, that *their sorrow was legitimate.* There was reason for their weeping. They saw Him suffering, friendless, and hunted to death, and they could not but bewail Him. Had I been there and seen Him all alone and marked the cruel eyes that watched Him and heard the malicious voices that assailed Him, I too must have wept. At least I hope I am not so past feeling as to have looked on without overflowing sorrow. See those bleeding shoulders, those lacerated temples—mark, above all, that quiet, unrivaled godlike countenance, so marred with sacred grief. One must have wept surely if one had a heart anywhere within him. And to think that He who suffered thus and was about to suffer so much more should be so gentle, so unresisting; was not this cause for intensest sympathy? He was meek and lowly in heart, and therefore He returned none of those fierce looks and answered none of those ferocious words. He was like a lamb in the midst of wolves or a dove surrounded by a thousand hawks or a fawn amid baying hounds. There was none to pity and none to help; shall we, then, refuse our compassion? Nay, the women's eyes did well to weep. How could they help it, since they were mothers of children and hence had hearts to love? How could they help weeping for Him who was so lowly, so gentle, so unselfish, so submissive to all the evil put upon Him? Surely it was the superfluity of malice to be hunting Him to death who even in life was so much the Man of sorrows.

And then withal He was so innocent and pure. What had He done wrong? They could not answer Pilate's challenge: "Why, what evil hath he done?" There was no fault in Him, they could not find any. You could see by the very look of Him that He was the purest of all mankind, that all around Him was sin and vanity, and He alone was holiness and truth. Wherefore, then, should they lead Him forth among malefactors and nail those blessed hands and feet to the wood and hang Him to a tree? Above all, in addition to His being innocent of fault He had been so full of kindness, of more than kindness—of infinite love to all mankind, and even in His deepest sorrow boundless benevolence shone in His countenance, beaming as the sun. He looked upon His enemies, and His glance was royal, but it was tender, too: "Father, forgive them, for they know not what they do" was trembling on His lips. He would not harm them, not He. He would not curse them, though His curse had withered them, nor even frown upon them, though that frown might have secured His liberation. He was too good to render evil for evil.

These women recollected what a life He had led. He had fed the hungry, perhaps some of them had even eaten of the loaves and fishes. He had healed their children, raised their dead, and dislodged evil spirits from the bodies of their friends. He had preached openly in their streets, and He had never taught ill will but always taught gentleness and love. He had been popular and had stood at the head of the multitude at one time, but He had never used His power for selfish purposes. He had ridden through their streets in pomp, but the pomp was simple and homely; on a colt, the foal of an ass, had He ridden with children for His courtiers, and with no sound of the trumpets of war but only with the children's cries of "Hosannah, blessed is he that cometh in the name of the Lord." Why should they crucify Him? He had done nothing but good. His noble presence seemed to appeal to women, and they asked each other, "For which of His works would they slay Him? For which of His actions would they put Him to death?" He, the Friend of the friendless, why should He die? I cannot, I say again, but commend the tears of these women. It is little marvel that they should weep and bewail when they saw the innocent one about to die.

I think, too, that *this weeping on the part of the women was a very hopeful emotion.* It was far better certainly than the nonemotion or the cruelty of those who formed that motley throng. It showed some tenderness of heart, and tenderness of heart, though it be but natural, may often serve as a foundation upon which better and holier and more spiritual feelings may be placed. It is objected that people weep when they hear the story of other griefs besides those of Jesus, and I am glad they do. Should they not weep with them that weep? It is also objected that this natural sympathy may in many cases be as much due to the skill of the orator as in others it is the undoubted result of the music of the oratorio. I know it is so.

I am going to show you that mere emotional sympathy is not all, nor a half, nor a tenth, of what is desired. Still I should be sorry if I thought myself capable of remembering the griefs of Jesus without emotion while other men's woes affected me. I should greatly deplore the fact if it were indeed true that you were so hardened that you could think of Jesus of Nazareth bleeding and dying without your heart beginning to melt.

The emotion is good at any rate so far that if it were absent you would be bereft of humanity and turned to stone. It is hopeful because it opens a door through which something better may enter. This tenderness is a natural stock suitable for grafting something far higher upon. He who can weep for the sorrows of Christ may soon be on the road toward weeping over the sin that caused the sorrow, or he may be on the highway toward being able to lament, as Christ bids men lament, those other griefs and miseries that sin brings upon themselves and upon their children. I would not carry the emotion toward Christ to an excess, nor ask men to make Jesus' death a fountain of sorrow only, since it is also a source of joy. I would deplore that idolatrous emotion that weeps before a hideous image or mourns over a touching picture. But still I would not have men act as if they were stones but prove that they mourn for Him whom they have pierced.

Having said this much, we now add that *on our Lord's part such sorrow was properly repressed,* because after all, though naturally good, it is not more than natural and falls short of spiritual excellence. It is no proof of the work of the Spirit upon your heart that you weep as you hear the story of Christ's death, for probably you would have been even more affected had you seen a murderer hanged. It is no proof that you are truly saved because you are moved to great emotions whenever you hear the details of the crucifixion, for the atrocities of war excite you equally as much. I think it good that you should be moved, as I have said before, but it is only natural and not spiritually good. Doubtless there are many who have shed more tears over the silly story of a lovesick man in a frivolous novel than they have ever given to the story of the Lover of our souls. Though they have felt emotion when they have pictured the sufferings of Emmanuel, they have felt even more when the bewitching pen of fiction had sketched some imaginary picture of fancied woes. No, no, these natural sympathies are not so to be commended that we wish you to be continually exercised with them. Our Lord did well to set them healthy bounds.

Besides, such feeling is generally very fleeting. Tears of mere emotion because of the external sufferings of Christ are speedily wiped away and forgotten. We do not know that any of these women ever became our Lord's converts. Among those who met in the upper room, we do not know that any had taken part with this company of weepers. These were women of Jerusalem, and the followers of Christ at His death, who ministered unto Him, were generally women from Galilee (Matt. 27:55–56). I fear that many of these Jerusalem sympathizers forgot tomorrow that they had wept today. I may be mistaken, but there is nothing in the mere fact of their lamenting the Savior's doom that proved them to be His regenerated followers. The morning cloud and the early dew are fit emblems of such fleeting emotions.

Such weeping too is morally powerless. It has no effect upon the mind. It does not change the character. It does not cause the putting away of sin or create real and saving faith in Jesus Christ. Many tears are shed under powerful sermons that are so much wasted fluid; the discourse is over, the sorrow has ceased. There was no work of grace upon the inner heart; it was all surface work and no more.

The worst of it is that such feeling is often deceptive, for people are apt to think, "I must have something good in me, for what a time of weeping I had under the sermon, and how tender I felt when I heard the description of Christ upon the cross!" Yes, and thus you may wrap yourself up in the belief that you are under the influence of the Holy Spirit when, after all, it is only ordinary human feeling. You may conclude, "Surely these drops flow from a heart of flesh," when it may be only moisture condensed upon a heart of stone.

This feeling, too, may stand in the way of something a great deal better. Jesus would not have these women weep for one thing because they were to weep for another thing that far more seriously demanded their weeping. You need not weep because Christ died one-tenth so much as because your sins rendered it necessary that He should die. You need not weep over the crucifixion, but weep over your transgression, for your sins nailed the Redeemer to the accursed tree. To weep over a dying Savior is to lament the remedy; it were wiser to bewail the disease. To weep over the dying Savior is to wet the surgeon's knife with tears; it were better to bewail the spreading cancer that the knife must cut away. To weep over the Lord Jesus as He goes to the cross is to weep over that which is the subject of the highest joy that ever heaven and earth have known. Your tears are scarcely needed there; they are natural, but a deeper wisdom will make you brush them all away and chant with joy His victory over death and the grave. If we must continue our sad emotions, let us lament that we should have broken the law that He thus painfully vindicated, let us mourn that we should have incurred the penalty that He even to the death was made to endure. Jesus wished them not so much to look at His outward sufferings as at the secret inward cause of that outward sorrow, namely, the transgression and the iniquity of His people, which had laid the cross upon His shoulders and surrounded Him with enemies. As I quoted certain verses that led us to lament our Lord, let me propose to you as better still those words of Watts:

> *'Twas you, my sins, my cruel sins,*
> *His chief tormentors were;*
> *Each of my crimes became a nail,*
> *And unbelief the spear.*

> *'Twas you that pull'd the vengeance down*
> *Upon His guiltless head:*
> *Break, break, my heart, oh burst mine eyes*
> *And let my sorrows bleed.*

> *Strike mighty grace, my flinty soul,*
> *Till melting waters flow,*
> *And deep repentance drown mine eyes*
> *In undissembled woe.*

## Weep

Now we pass on from "weep not" to "weep." May God the Holy Spirit help us to dwell upon that for a while with profit to our souls. Though Jesus stops one channel for tears, He opens another and a wider one. Let us look to it.

First, when He said, "Weep for yourselves," he meant that *they were to lament and bewail the sin that had brought Him where He was,* seeing He had come to suffer for it. He would have them weep because that sin would bring them and their children into yet deeper woe. You know that just before He uttered this remarkable saying the husbands, and the fathers, and the sons of those women had been crying with loud voices, "Let Him be crucified." And when Pilate had taken water and washed his hands to show that he was innocent of the blood of Jesus, they had imprecated upon their nation and upon their unborn sons the curse that follows from such a deed. "Then answered all the people, and said, His blood be on us, and on our children" (Matt. 27:25). Though these women lamented and mourned, yet over their heads the men who had spoken for the nation had gathered the thundercloud of divine wrath. Jesus points to it and says, "Weep for the national sin, weep for the national curse, that will surely come upon you, because you are putting the just One to death."

Yea, deeper still was His meaning, for all those about Him were in a sense guilty of His death. And you and I and all the rest of mankind have been, in our measure, the cause of the Savior's crucifixion. This is the reason why we should weep, because we have broken the divine law and rendered it impossible that we should be saved except Jesus Christ should die. If we have not believed in Jesus Christ, we have this cause for lamentation, that our sin abides upon us at this present moment. The curse that crushed the Savior down till He said *Eloi, Eloi, lama, sabachthani* is resting upon some who are reading these words. O souls, you need not pity the dying Christ, but pity yourselves. On your own selves your sin is resting, and your children growing up unconverted, hardened in rebellion against God by your example. Their sin is resting upon them, too, and this is the overflowing cause why you should weep. And you believers, you from whom sin has been lifted, who are forgiven for His name's sake, yet lament that you should have sinned, and with your joy for pardoned guilt mourn that Christ had to carry the burden that you deserved. All around there is abounding cause for sorrow for sin—a sweet sorrow from the Lord's people and a bitter sorrow from those who have no part or lot in the result of Christ's passion as yet but who nevertheless are partakers in the crime that slew the Son of God.

I beg you now to look again into the reason why our Lord bade them weep. It was, first, for their sin, but it was next *for the impending punishment of their sins.* The punishment of the national sin of the Jew was to be the scattering of his nation and the total destruction of its holy city. Well does our Savior speak of it in terrible language, for under all heaven and in all history there never was such a scene of misery as the siege and destruction of Jerusalem. Nothing has ever surpassed it. I question whether anything ever equaled it. But our Lord, as I have hinted, looked further than the Roman sword and the massacre of the Jews. Often in His preaching you do not know whether He is talking of the siege of Jerusalem or of the judgment day, for the one was in His mind such a foreshadowing, rehearsal, and type of the other that in His language He often seemed to melt the two into one.

He means to you and to me to speak not of besieged Jerusalem but of that day of wrath, that dreadful day, whose coming what man among us shall be able to abide? Concerning that there is cause enough for weeping, for when that day comes it would have been better for them that they had never been born. When the dreadful sentence shall come from the Judge, "Depart from me, ye cursed, into everlasting fire, prepared for the devil and his angels" (Matt. 25:41), they will bless the barren womb and the breast at which no child has sucked. Then will impenitent sinners bitterly exclaim, "Cursed be the day wherein I was born: let not the day wherein my mother bare me be blessed. Cursed be the man who brought tidings to my father, saying, A man child is born unto thee; making him very glad" (Jer. 20:14–15). They will wring their hands in anguish and curse their existence and wish that they had never seen the light. So terrible will the doom of the wicked be that mothers who looked upon the birth of their children as the consummation of their joy shall wish they had been barren and never carried a babe at their breast. Existence is in itself a blessing, but what shall be the misery that shall make men wish that they had never breathed? Yet, alas, such is the condition of many to whom I am writing, and such will soon be the condition of some who are reading these words now, except they repent! Alas! Alas! Weep for yourselves and for your children!

Further, our Lord went on, with that melting voice of His, in overflowing grief to say that they might reserve their tears for those who would soon desire to be annihilated but wish in vain. "Then shall men begin to say to the mountains, fall on us, and to the hills, cover us." The falling of the mountain would grind them to powder, and they wish for that. The descent of the hill upon them would bury them in a deep abyss, and they would rather be immured in the bowels of the earth forever than have to look upon the face of the great Judge. They ask to be crushed outright or to be buried alive sooner than to feel the punishment of their sins. Then shall be fulfilled the word of the Lord by His servant John: "And in those days shall men seek death, and shall not find it; and shall desire to die, and death shall flee from them" (Rev. 9:6). Ah, extinction is a privilege too great to be permitted to the ungodly. Earth will have no bowels of compassion for the men who polluted her and rejected her Lord.

The mountains will reply, "We fall at God's bidding, not at the petition of His enemies." And the hills in their stolid silence will answer, "We cannot, and we would not if we could, conceal you from the justice that you yourselves willfully provoked." No, there shall be no refuge for them, no annihilation into which they can fly. The very hope of it were heaven to the damned. Their cry for extinction shall be in vain. Now, if you have tears for Jesus' dying, reserve them for those to whom death is but the beginning of evils! If you have griefs for Him to whom they said "Blessed is the womb that bare thee, and the paps that gave thee suck," have still more tears for those who shall curse the hour in which they were conceived. Here is indeed a subject that demands the tears of nations and of ages—souls lost beyond all remedy, seeking destruction itself as a blessing, and *beginning* petitions of unutterable anguish that shall never cease and never avail.

Then our Lord goes on to draw *a wonderful parallel and contrast between His sufferings and those to be lamented,* for He says, "If they do these things in a green tree, what shall they do in the dry?" I suppose He meant, "If I, who am no rebel against Caesar, suffer so, how will those suffer whom the Romans take in actual rebellion at the siege of Jerusalem?" And He meant next to say, "If I who am perfectly innocent, must nevertheless be put to such a death as this, what will become of the guilty?" If, when fires are raging in the forest, the green trees full of sap and moisture crackle like stubble in the flame, how will the old dry trees burn that are already rotten to the core, and turned to touchwood, and so prepared as fuel for the furnace. If Jesus suffers who has no sin but is full of the life of innocence and the sap of holiness, how will they suffer who have long been dead in sin and are rotten with iniquity? As Peter puts it in another place, "For the time is come that judgment must begin at the house of God: and if it first begin at us, what shall be the end of them that obey not the gospel of God? And if the righteous scarcely be saved, where shall the ungodly and the sinner appear?" (1 Pet. 4:17–18).

Note well that the sufferings of our Lord, though in some respects far beyond all conceivable woes, have yet some points about them in which they differ with advantage from the miseries of lost souls. First, our Lord knew that He was innocent, and therefore His righteousness upheld Him. Whatever He suffered He knew that He deserved none of it. He had no stings of conscience nor agonies of remorse. Now, the sting of future punishment will lie in the indisputable conviction that it is well deserved. If there were one woe in hell more than a lost soul deserved, it would act as an opiate to its pain, but the justice of every infliction will be the tooth of the worm, the edge of the sword. No dream of innocence or conceit of self-righteousness will survive the judgment day, but conscience will be aroused and armed to do its work. The wicked will perceive their guilt and cling to it, and this will make their punishment the more severe.

The finally impenitent will be tormented by their own passions that will rage within them like an inward hell, but our Lord had none of this. There was no evil in Him, no lusting after evil, no self-seeking, no rebellion of heart, no anger, or discontent. A man in whom there is no evil passion to stir up cannot know those fierce pangs and wild throes with which raging sin rends the soul. Pride, ambition, greed, malice, revenge—these are the fuel of hell's fire. Men's selves, not devils, are their tormentors—their inward lusts are worms that never die and fires that never can be quenched. There could be none of this in our divine Lord. Again, lost souls hate God and love sin, but Christ ever loved God and hated sin. Now, to love evil is misery. When undisguised and rightly understood, sin is hell, and it is love of evil continued in the soul that causes the perpetuity of the lost estate of men. But the holy Jesus, though suffering beyond all conception, could not feel the pangs that come of hating good and loving evil. He was the green tree, and the ungodly are the dry trees. Yet if the innocent One suffer so, with what pains will guilty souls be racked by their avenging consciences.

Our Lord Jesus knew that every pang He suffered was for the good of others. He endured cheerfully because He saw that He was redeeming a multitude that no man can number from going down to the pit. But there is no redeeming power about the sufferings of the lost; they are not helping anyone, nor are they achieving a benevolent design. The great God has good designs in their punishment, but they are strangers to any such purpose.

Our Lord had a reward before Him, because of which He endured the cross, despising the shame; but the finally condemned have no prospect of reward or hope of rising from their doom. How can they expect either? *He* was full of hope; *they* are full of despair. "It is finished" was for Him, but there is no "It is finished" for them.

Their sufferings, moreover, are self-caused; their sin was their own. Jesus endured agonies because others had transgressed, and He willed to save them. Their sufferings are self-chosen, for they would not be persuaded to forsake their sins. But He, from necessity of love, was made to bleed—the cup could not pass from Him if His people were redeemed. The torments of the lost will be self-inflicted. They are suicides to their souls, the venom in their veins themselves with sin, to which they cleave; but it pleased the Father to bruise the Son, and the necessity for His bruising lay not in Himself but in others.

Now, dear friend, I think I have said enough on this painful matter to assure you that the most terrible warning to impenitent men in all the world is the death of Christ, for if God spared not His own Son, on whom was only laid imputed sin, will He spare sinners whose sins are actual and their own? If He smote Him to the death who only stood in the sinner's stead, will He let the impenitent sinner go free? If He who always did His Father's will and was obedient even unto death must be forsaken of God, what will become of those who reject Christ and live and die enemies to the Most High? Here is cause for weeping, and very solemnly would I say it—God help me to say it so that you may feel it—the most dreadful thought is that perhaps we ourselves are in the condition of guiltiness before God and are hastening on to the judgment that Christ has foretold. Think if within the next six months—nay, stretch it as far as you like—if within the next fifty years, some of us should be asking the hills to cover us and wishing that we had never been born. What an awful prospect! And yet, unless we are renewed in heart and made believers in Jesus Christ, that certainly must be our doom. Think of your children, too, who are growing up about you, capable of understanding and responsible for their actions. If they live as they now live and die as they now are, you may wish that they had never been given to you and had never borne your name. Think of this and weep. Dear friend, if the Lord would put you into a right state of heart, you would scarcely think of an unconverted person's condition without the deepest pity. You would not hear a foul word in the street without the tear starting to your eye.

That was a dreadful spectacle that I pictured to you just now— our Lord bearing His cross and the women weeping. But how much more awful is that before me! I see a soul carrying about itself the instrument of its own destruction and going onward to its doom! Sin is the cross to which the soul will be fastened, and habits and depravities are the nails. The soul is bearing its sin and loving to bear it. See, it is going to execution, but at each step it laughs. Every step it takes is bearing it toward hell, and yet it makes mirth! Lo, the infatuated one scoffs at the voice that warns him, and every scoff he utters is increasing his guilt. Look forward to his end, its never-ending end. Look forward to it steadily, with calm and tearful gaze. Is it not an awful spectacle? But what if you should be beholding yourself as in a vision or seeing your child in the glass of prophecy! If it be your case, I beseech you repent of your sin, bewail your condition, and fly to Christ for shelter. And if it is your child, give heaven no rest, plead continually at the throne of grace till you have brought down a blessing from God upon your off-spring. Never cease to pray until your sons and your daughters are safe landed on the Rock of Ages and so secured there they will need no other rock to hide them in the day when Christ shall come. I beseech you, ask for tenderness toward sinners, toward all sinners, and let your tenderness be shown in fervent prayer, in incessant effort, and in holy sympathy toward the wandering ones.

Alas, I have but stuttered and stammered compared with the manner in which I hoped to have written. I may have failed in expressing myself, but God can bless the word nonetheless. The subject is worthy of an angel's tongue; it needs Christ Himself completely to expound it. Would God He might by His own Spirit expound it to your heart.

*I* love this prayer, also, because of the indistinctness of it. It is "Father, forgive them." Jesus does not say, "Father, forgive the soldiers who have nailed Me here." He includes them. Neither does He say, "Father, forgive the people who are beholding Me." He means them. Neither does He say, "Father, forgive sinners in ages to come who will sin against Me." But He means them. Jesus does not mention them by any accusing name: "Father, forgive My enemies. Father, forgive My murderers." No, there is no word of accusation upon those dear lips. "Father, forgive them." Now into that pronoun them I feel that I can crawl. Can you get in there? Oh, by a humble faith, appropriate the cross of Christ by trusting in it, and get into that big little word them! It seems like a chariot of mercy that has come down to earth, into which a man may step, and it shall bear him up to heaven. "Father, forgive them."

# Chapter Four

# Christ's Plea
# for Ignorant Sinners

*Then said Jesus, Father, forgive them; for they know not what they do*—Luke 23:34.

WHAT TENDERNESS WE HAVE here, what self-forgetfulness, what almighty love! Jesus did not say to those who crucified Him, "Begone!" One such word, and they must have all fled. When they came to take Him in the garden, they went backward and fell to the ground when He spoke but a short sentence. And now that He is on the cross, a single syllable would have made the whole company fall to the ground or flee away in fright.

Jesus says not a word in His own defense. When He prayed to His Father, He might justly have said, "Father, note what they do to your beloved Son. Judge them for the wrong they do to Him who loves them, and who has done all He can for them." But there is no prayer against them in the words that Jesus utters. It was written of old, by the prophet Isaiah, "[He] made intercession for the transgressors" (53:12); and here it is fulfilled. He pleads for His murderers, "Father, forgive them."

He does not utter a single word of upbraiding. He does not say, "Why do you do this? Why pierce the hands that fed you? Why nail the feet that followed after you in mercy? Why mock the Man who loved to bless you?" No; not a word even of gentle upbraiding, much less of anything like a curse. "Father, forgive them." You notice, Jesus does not say, "I forgive them," but you may read that between the lines. He says that all the more because He does not say it in words. But He has laid aside His majesty and is nailed to the cross, and therefore He takes the humble position of a suppliant rather than the more lofty place of one who has power to forgive. How often, when men say, "I forgive you," is there a kind of selfishness about it! At any rate, self is asserted in the very act of forgiving. Jesus takes the place of a pleader, a pleader for those who were committing murder upon Him. Blessed be His name!

This word of the cross we shall use, and we shall see whether we cannot gather something from it for our instruction. For though we were not there and we did not actually put Jesus to death, yet we really caused His death, and we, too, crucified the Lord of glory. His prayer for us was, "Father, forgive them; for they know not what they do."

I am not going to handle this text so much by way of exposition as by way of experience. I believe there are many readers to whom these words will be very appropriate. This will be our line of thought. First, *we were in measure ignorant*. Second, *we confess that this ignorance is no excuse*. Third, *we bless our Lord for pleading for us*. And fourth, *we now rejoice in the pardon we have obtained*. May the Holy Spirit graciously help us in our meditation.

## We Were in Measure Ignorant

Looking back upon our past experience, let me say, first, that we were in measure ignorant. We who have been forgiven, we who have been washed in the blood of the Lamb, we once sinned, in a great measure, through ignorance. Jesus says, "They know not what they do." Now, I shall appeal to you. When you lived under the dominion of Satan and served yourselves and sin, was there not a measure of ignorance in it? You can truly say, as we sing in the hymn, "Alas, I knew not what I did!"

It is true, first, that we were ignorant of *the awful meaning of sin*. We began to sin as children. We knew that it was wrong, but we did not know all that sin meant. We went on to sin as young men and women, and perhaps we plunged into much wickedness. We knew it was wrong, but we did not see the end from the beginning. It did not appear to us as rebellion against God. We did not think that we were presumptuously defying God, setting at naught His wisdom, defying His power, deriding His love, spurning His holiness; yet we were doing all that. There is an abysmal depth in sin. You cannot see to the bottom of it. When we rolled sin under our tongue as a sweet morsel, we did not know all the terrible ingredients compounded in that deadly bittersweet. We were in a measure ignorant of the tremendous crime we committed when we dared to live in rebellion against God. So far, I think, you will agree with me.

We did not know, at that time, *God's great love for us.* I did not know that He had chosen me from before the foundation of the world. I never dreamed of that. I did not know that Christ stood for me as my Substitute, to redeem me from among men. I did not know that He had espoused me unto Himself in righteousness and in faithfulness, to be one with Him forever. You, dear friends, who now know the love of Christ, did not understand it then. You did not know that you were sinning against eternal love, against infinite compassion, against a distinguishing love such as God had fixed on you from eternity. So far, we knew not what we did.

I think, too, that we did not know all that we were doing in *our rejection of Christ and putting Him to grief.* He came to us in our youth, and impressed by a sermon, we began to tremble and to seek His face. But we were decoyed back to the world and refused Christ. Our mother's tears, our father's prayers, our teacher's admonitions often moved us. But we were very stubborn, and we rejected Christ. We did not know that in that rejection, we were virtually putting Him away and crucifying Him. We were denying His Godhead, or else we should have worshiped Him. We were denying His love, or else we should have yielded to Him. We were practically, in every act of sin, taking the hammer and the nails and fastening Christ to the cross. But we did not know it. Perhaps, if we had known it, we should not have crucified the Lord of glory. We did know we were doing wrong, but we did not know all the wrong that we were doing.

Nor did we know fully *the meaning of our delays.* We hesitated when we were on the verge of conversion; we went back and turned again to our old follies. We were hardened, Christless, prayerless still, and each one of us said, "Oh, I am only waiting a little while till I have fulfilled my present engagements, till I am a little older, till I have seen a little more of the world!" The fact is, we were refusing Christ and choosing the pleasures of sin instead of Him. Every hour of delay was an hour of crucifying Christ, grieving His Spirit, and choosing this harlot world in the place of the lovely and ever-blessed Christ. We did not know that.

I think we may add one thing more. *We did not know the meaning of our self-righteousness.* We used to think, some of us, that we had a righteousness of our own. We had been to church regularly. We were christened; we were confirmed; or, perhaps, we rejoiced that we never had either of those things done to us. Thus, we put our confidence in ceremonies or the absence of ceremonies. We said our prayers; we read a chapter in the Bible night and morning; we did—oh, I do not know what we did not do! But there we rested as righteous in our own esteem. We had not any particular sin to confess nor any reason to lie in the dust before the throne of God's majesty. We were about as good as we could be, and we did not know that we were even then perpetrating the highest insult upon Christ. For if we were not sinners, why did Christ die? If we had a righteousness of our own that was good enough, why did Christ come here to work out a righteousness for us? We made out Christ to be a superfluity by considering that we were good enough without resting in His atoning sacrifice. Ah, we did not think we were doing that! We thought we were pleasing God by our religiousness, by our outward performances, by our ecclesiastical correctness. But all the while we were setting up antichrist in the place of Christ. We were making out that Christ was not needed. We were robbing Him of His office and glory! Alas! Christ could say of us, with regard to all these things, "They know not what they do." I want you to look quietly at the time past wherein you served sin and see whether there was not a darkness upon your mind, a blindness in your spirit, so that you did not know what you did.

## We Confess That This Ignorance Is No Excuse

Our Lord might urge our ignorance as a plea, but we never could. We did not know what we did, and so we were not guilty to the fullest possible extent. But we were guilty enough; therefore, let us own it.

For first, remember, *the law never allows this as a plea*. In our own English law, a man is supposed to know what the law is. If he breaks it, it is no excuse to plead that he did not know it. It may be regarded by a judge as some extenuation, but the law allows nothing of the kind. God gives us the law, and we are bound to keep it. If I erred through not knowing the law, still it was a sin. Under the

Mosaic law, there were sins of ignorance, and for these there were special offerings. The ignorance did not blot out the sin. That is clear in my text, for if ignorance rendered an action no longer sinful, why should Christ say, "Father, forgive them"? But He does. He asks for mercy for what is sin, even though the ignorance in some measure is supposed to mitigate the criminality of it.

But, dear friend, *we might have known.* If we did not know, it was because we would not know. There was the preaching of the Word, but we did not care to hear it. There was this blessed Book, but we did not care to read it. If you and I had sat down and looked at our conduct by the light of Holy Scripture, we might have known much more of the evil of sin, and much more of the love of Christ, and much more of the ingratitude that is possible in refusing Christ and not coming to Him.

In addition to that, *we did not think.* "Oh, but," you say, "young people never do think!" But young people should think. If there is anybody who need not think, it is the old man, whose day is nearly over. If he does think, he has but a very short time in which to improve. But the young have all their life before them. If I were a carpenter and had to make a box, I should not think about it after I had made the box. I should think, before I began to cut my timber, what sort of box it was to be. In every action, a man thinks before he begins, or else he is a fool. A young man should think more than anybody else, for now he is, as it were, making his box. Because he is beginning his life plan, he should be the most thoughtful of all men. Many of us who are now Christ's people would have known much more about our Lord if we had given Him more careful consideration in our earlier days. A man will consider about taking a wife, he will consider about taking a business, he will consider about buying a horse or a cow, but he will not consider about the claims of Christ and the claims of the Most High God. This renders his ignorance willful and inexcusable.

Beside that, dear friend, although we have confessed to ignorance, *in many sins we did know a great deal.* Come, let me quicken your memories. There were times when you knew that such an action was wrong when you started back from it. You looked at the gain it would bring you, and you sold your soul for that price and deliberately did what you were well aware was wrong. Are there not some readers saved by Christ who must confess that at times they did violence to their conscience? They did despite to the Spirit of God, quenched the light of heaven, drove the Spirit away from them, distinctly knowing what they were doing. Let us bow before God in the silence of our hearts and own to all this. We hear the Master say, "Father, forgive them; for they know not what they do." Let us add our own tears as we say, "And forgive us, also, because in some things we did know; in all things we might have known, but we were ignorant for lack of thought, which thought was a solemn duty that we should have rendered to God."

One thing more I will say on this point. When a man is ignorant and does not know what he ought to do, what should he do? Well, he should do nothing till he does know. But here is the mischief of it, that *when we did not know, yet we chose to do the wrong thing.* If we did not know, why did we not choose the right thing? But being in the dark, we never turned to the right but always blundered to the left, from sin to sin. Does not this show us how depraved our hearts are? Though we are seeking to be right, when we are let alone, we go wrong of ourselves. Let a child alone; let a man alone; let a group alone without teaching and instruction; what comes of it? Why, the same as when you let a field alone. It never, by any chance, produces wheat or barley. Let it alone, and there are rank weeds, thorns, and briars, showing that the natural set of the soil is toward producing that which is worthless. O friend, confess the innate evil of your heart as well as the evil of your life, in that when you did not know, yet, having a perverse instinct, you chose the evil and refused the good. When you did not know enough of Christ and did not think enough of Him to know whether you should have Him or not, you would not come to Him that you might have life. You needed light, but you shut your eyes to the sun. You were thirsty, but you would not drink of the living spring. And so your ignorance, though it was there, was a criminal ignorance that you must confess before the Lord. Oh, come to the cross, you who have been there before and have lost your burden there! Come and confess your guilt over again, and grasp that cross afresh, and look to Him who bled upon it, and praise His dear name that He once prayed for you, "Father, forgive them, for they know not what they do."

Now, I am going a step further. We were in a measure ignorant, but we confess that the measurable ignorance was no excuse.

## We Bless Our Lord for Pleading for Us

Do you notice when it was that Jesus pleaded? It was *while they were crucifying Him.* They had just driven in the nails; they had lifted up the cross and dashed it down into its socket, dislocating all His bones, so that He could say, "I am poured out like water, and all my bones are out of joint" (Ps. 22:14). Ah, dear friend, it was then that instead of a cry or a groan, this dear Son of God said, "Father, forgive them; for they know not what they do." They did not ask forgiveness for themselves, but Jesus asked forgiveness for them. When their hands were imbrued in His blood, it was then, even then, that He prayed for them. Let us think of the great love wherewith He loved us, even while we were yet sinners, when we rioted in sin, when we drank it down as the ox drinks down water. Even then He prayed for us. "For when we were yet without strength, in due time Christ died for the ungodly" (Rom. 5:6). Bless His name. He prayed for you when you did not pray for yourself. He prayed for you when you were crucifying Him.

Then think of His plea—*He pleads His Sonship.* He says, "Father, forgive them." He was the Son of God, and He puts His divine Sonship into the scale on our behalf. He seems to say, "Father, as I am your Son, grant Me this request and pardon these rebels. Father, forgive them." The filial rights of Christ were very great. He was the Son of God, not as we are, by adoption, but by nature. By eternal filiation, He was the Son of the Highest, "Light of light, very God of very God," the second person in the divine trinity. And He puts that Sonship here before God and says, "Father, Father, forgive them." Oh, the power of that word from the Son's lips when He is wounded, when He is in agony, when He is dying! He says, "Father, Father, grant My one request. O Father, forgive them, for they know not what they do." And the great Father bows His majestic head, in token that the petition is granted.

Then notice that Jesus here, silently, but really *pleads His sufferings.* The attitude of Christ when He prayed this prayer is very noteworthy. His hands were stretched upon the transverse beam, His feet were fastened to the upright tree, and there He pleaded. Silently His hands and feet were pleading, and His agonized body from every sinew and muscle pleaded with God. His sacrifice was presented there before the Father's face—not yet complete but in His will complete. And so it is His cross that takes up the plea: "Father, forgive them." O blessed Christ! It is thus that we have been forgiven, for His Sonship and His cross have pleaded with God and have prevailed on our behalf.

I love this prayer, also, because of the *indistinctness* of it. It is "Father, forgive *them*." Jesus does not say, "Father, forgive the soldiers who have nailed Me here." He includes them. Neither does He say, "Father, forgive the people who are beholding Me." He means them. Neither does He say, "Father, forgive sinners in ages to come who will sin against Me." But He means them. Jesus does not mention them by any accusing name: "Father, forgive My enemies. Father, forgive My murderers." No, there is no word of accusation upon those dear lips. "Father, forgive them." Now into that pronoun *them* I feel that I can crawl. Can you get in there? Oh, by a humble faith, appropriate the cross of Christ by trusting in it, and get into that big little word *them*! It seems like a chariot of mercy that has come down to earth, into which a man may step, and it shall bear him up to heaven. "Father, forgive them."

Notice, also, what it was that Jesus asked for; to omit that would be to leave out the very essence of His prayer. *He asked for full absolution for His enemies:* "Father, forgive them. Do not punish them; forgive them. Do not remember their sin; forgive it, blot it out; throw it into the depths of the sea. Remember it not, My Father. Mention it not against them anymore forever. Father, forgive them." Oh, blessed prayer, for the forgiveness of God is broad and deep! When man forgives, he leaves remembrance of the wrong behind. But when God pardons, He says, "I will forgive their iniquity, and I will remember their sin no more" (Jer. 31:34). It is this that Christ asked for you and me long before we had any repentance or any faith. In answer to that prayer, we were brought to feel our sin, we were brought to confess it and to believe in Him. And now, glory be to His name, we can bless Him for having pleaded for us and obtained the forgiveness of all our sins.

## We Now Rejoice in the Pardon We Have Obtained

Have you obtained pardon? Is this your song?

> *Now, oh joy! my sins are pardon'd,*
> *Now I can, and do believe.*

I have a letter in my pocket from a man of education and standing who was an agnostic. He says that he was a sarcastic agnostic, and he writes praising God and invoking every blessing upon my head for bringing him to the Savior's feet. He says, "I was without happiness for this life, and without hope for the next." I believe that that is a truthful description of many unbelievers. Apart from the cross of Christ, what hope is there for the world to come? The best hope such a man has is that he may die the death of a dog and there may be an end of him. I do not know of any religion but that of Christ Jesus that tells us of sin pardoned, absolutely pardoned. Now, listen. Our teaching is not that when you come to die, you may, perhaps, find out that it is all right, but, "Beloved, now are we the sons of God" (1 John 3:2). "He that believeth on the Son hath everlasting life" (John 3:36). He has it now, and he knows it, and he rejoices in it. So I come back to the last point of my discourse; we rejoice in the pardon Christ has obtained for us. We are pardoned. I hope that the larger portion of my readers can say, "By the grace of God, we know that we are washed in the blood of the Lamb."

*Pardon has come to us through Christ's plea.* Our hope lies in the plea of Christ and especially in His death. If Jesus paid my debt, and He did if I am a believer in Him, then I am out of debt. If Jesus bore the penalty of my sin, and He did if I am a believer, then there is no penalty for me to pay, for we can say to Him:

> *Complete atonement Thou hast made,*
> *And to the utmost farthing paid*
> *Whate'er Thy people owed:*
> *Nor can His wrath on me take place,*
> *If shelter'd in Thy righteousness,*
> *And sprinkled with Thy blood.*
>
> *If Thou hast my discharge procured,*
> *And freely in my room endured*
> *The whole of wrath divine:*
> *Payment God cannot twice demand,*
> *First at my bleeding Surety's hand,*
> *And then again at mine.*

If Christ has borne my punishment, I shall never bear it. Oh, what joy there is in this blessed assurance! Your hope that you are pardoned lies in this, that Jesus died. Those dear wounds of His bleed life for you.

We have praised Him for our pardon because *we do know now what we did.* O brethren, I know not how much we should love

Christ, because we sinned against Him so grievously! Now we know that sin is "exceeding sinful." Now we know that sin crucified Christ. Now we know that we stabbed our heavenly Lover to His heart. We slew with ignominious death our best and dearest Friend and Benefactor. We know that now, and we could almost weep tears of blood to think that we ever treated Him as we did. But it is all forgiven, all gone. Oh, let us bless that dear Son of God who has put away even such sins as ours! We feel them more now than ever before. We know they are forgiven, and our grief is because of the pain that the purchase of our forgiveness cost our Savior. We never knew what our sins really were till we saw Him in a bloody sweat. We never knew the crimson hue of our sins till we read our pardon written in crimson lines with His precious blood. Now we see our sin, and yet we do not see it, for God has pardoned it, blotted it out, cast it behind His back forever.

Henceforth, *ignorance* such as we have described *shall be hateful to us.* Ignorance of Christ and eternal things shall be hateful to us. If, through ignorance, we have sinned, we will have done with that ignorance. We will be students of His Word. We will study that masterpiece of all the sciences, the knowledge of Christ crucified. We will ask the Holy Ghost to drive far from us the ignorance that produces sin. God grant that we may not fall into sins of ignorance anymore. But may we be able to say, "I know whom I have believed, and henceforth I will seek more knowledge till I comprehend, with all saints, what are the heights, and depths, and lengths, and breadths of the love of Christ, and know the love of God, which passeth knowledge."

I will put in a practical word here. If you rejoice that you are pardoned, *show your gratitude by your imitation of Christ.* There was never before such a plea as this, "Father, forgive them; for they know not what they do." Plead like that for others. Has anybody been injuring you? Are there persons who slander you? Pray, "Father, forgive them; for they know not what they do." Let us always render good for evil, blessing for cursing. When we are called to suffer through the wrongdoings of others, let us believe that they would not act as they do if it were not because of their ignorance. Let us pray for them and make their very ignorance the plea for their forgiveness: "Father, forgive them, for they know not what they do."

I want you also to think of the millions around you. See those miles of streets pouring out their children this evening. But look at those taverns and night places with the crowds streaming in and out. Go down your streets by moonlight. See what I almost blush to tell. Follow men and women, too, to their homes, and be this your prayer: "Father, forgive them; for they know not what they do." That silver bell—keep it always ringing. What did I say? That silver bell? Nay, it is the *golden* bell upon the Priest's garments. Wear it on your garments, you priests of God, and let it always ring out its golden note, "Father, forgive them; for they know not what they do." If I can set all God's saints imitating Christ with such a prayer as this, I shall not have spoken in vain.

Brethren, I see *reason for hope in the very ignorance that surrounds us*. I see hope for this poor city of ours, hope for this poor country, hope for Africa, China, and India. "They know not what they do." Here is a strong argument in their favor, for they are more ignorant than we were. They know less of the evil of sin and less of the hope of eternal life than we do. Send up this petition, you people of God! Heap your prayers together with cumulative power, send up this fiery shaft of prayer, straight to the heart of God, while Jesus from His throne shall add His prevalent intercession, "Father, forgive them; for they know not what they do."

*O*bserve, that this man believed in Christ when he literally saw Him dying the death of a felon, under circumstances of the greatest personal shame. You have never realized what it was to be crucified. None of you could do that, for the sight has never been seen in our day in England. There is not a man or woman here who has ever realized in his or her own mind the actual death of Christ. It stands beyond us. This man saw it with his own eyes, and for him to call Him "Lord" who was hanging on a gibbet was no small triumph of faith. For him to ask Jesus to remember him when He came into His kingdom, though he saw that Jesus bleeding His life away and hounded to the death, was a splendid act of reliance. For him to commit his everlasting destiny into the hands of One who was, to all appearance, unable even to preserve His own life was a noble achievement of faith. I say that this dying thief leads the way in the matter of faith, for what he saw of the circumstances of the Savior was calculated to contradict rather than help his confidence. What he saw was to his hindrance rather than to his help, for he saw our Lord in the very extremity of agony and death, and yet he believed in Him as the King shortly to come to His kingdom.

## Chapter Five

# The Dying Thief
# in a New Light

*But the other answering rebuked him, saying, Dost not thou fear God, seeing thou art in the same condemnation? And we indeed justly; for we receive the due reward of our deeds: but this man hath done nothing amiss. And he said unto Jesus, Lord, remember me when thou comest into thy kingdom.*—Luke 23:40–42.

A GREAT MANY PERSONS, whenever they hear of the conversion of the dying thief, remember that he was saved in the very act of death, and they dwell upon that fact, and that alone. He has always been quoted as a case of salvation at the eleventh hour, and so, indeed, he is. In his case it is proven that as long as a man can repent, he can obtain forgiveness. The cross of Christ avails even for a man hanging on a gibbet and drawing near to his last hour. He who is mighty to save was mighty, even during His own death, to pluck others from the grasp of the destroyer, though they were in the act of expiring.

But that is not everything that the story teaches us. It is always a pity to look exclusively upon one point and thus to miss everything else—perhaps miss that which is more important. So often has this been the case that it has produced a sort of revulsion of feeling in certain minds, so that they have been driven in a wrong direction by their wish to protest against what they think to be a common error. I read the other day that this story of the dying thief should not be taken as an encouragement to deathbed repentance. Brethren, if the author meant—and I do not think he did mean— that this should never be used to lead people to postpone repentance to a dying bed, he spoke correctly. No Christian man could or would use it so injuriously: He must be hopelessly bad who would draw from God's long-suffering an argument for continuing in sin.

I trust, however, that the narrative is seldom used in this way, even by the worst of men. It cannot be properly turned to such a purpose. It might be used as an encouragement to thieving just as much as to the delay of repentance. I might say, "I may be a thief because this thief was saved," just as rationally as I might say, "I may put off repentance because this thief was saved when he was about to die." The fact is there is nothing so good but men can pervert it into evil if they have evil hearts. The justice of God is made a motive for despair and His mercy an argument for sin. Wicked men will drown themselves in the rivers of truth as readily as in the pools of error. He who has a mind to destroy himself can choke his soul with the Bread of Life or dash himself in pieces against the Rock of Ages. There is no doctrine of the grace of God so gracious that graceless men may not turn it into licentiousness.

I venture, however, to say that if I stood by the bedside of a dying man tonight and I found him anxious about his soul but fearful that Christ could not save him because repentance had been put off so late, I should certainly quote the dying thief to him, and I should do it with good conscience and without hesitation. I should tell him that though he was as near to dying as the thief upon the cross was, yet, if he repented of his sin and turned his face to Christ believingly, he would find eternal life. I should do this with all my heart, rejoicing that I had such a story to tell to one at the gates of eternity. I do not think that I should be censured by the Holy Spirit for thus using a narrative that He has Himself recorded—recorded with the foresight in my own heart, a sweet conviction that I had treated the subject as I should have treated it, and as it was intended to be used for men *in extremis* whose hearts are turning toward the living God. Oh, yes, poor soul, whatever your age or whatever the period of life to which you have come, you may now find eternal life by faith in Christ!

> *The dying thief rejoiced to see*
> *That fountain in his day;*

*And there may you, though vile as he,*
*Wash all your sins away.*

Many good people think that they ought to guard the gospel, but it is never so safe as when it stands out in its own naked majesty. It needs no covering from us. When we protect it with conditions and guard it with exceptions and qualify it with observations, it is like David in Saul's armor: It is hampered and hindered, and you may even hear it cry, "I cannot go with these." Let the gospel alone, and it will save. Qualify it, and the salt has lost its savor. I will venture to put it thus to you. I have heard it said that few are ever converted in old age, and this is thought to be a statement that will prove exceedingly arousing and impressive for the young. It certainly seems to be true. On the other hand, it is a statement very discouraging to the old. I demur to the frequent repetition of such statements, for I do not find their counterpart in the teaching of our Lord and His apostles. Assuredly our Lord spoke of some who entered the vineyard at the eleventh hour of the day, and among His miracles He not only saved those who were dying but also even raised the dead.

Nothing can be concluded from the words of the Lord Jesus against the salvation of men at any hour or age. I tell you that in the business of your acceptance with God through faith in Christ Jesus, it does not matter what age you now are. The same promise is to every one of you: "To day if ye will hear His voice, harden not your hearts" (Heb. 3:15, 4:7). Whether you are in the earliest stage of life or are within a few hours of eternity, if now you fly for refuge to the hope set before you in the gospel, you shall be saved. The gospel that I preach excludes none on the ground either of age or character. Whoever you may be, "Believe on the Lord Jesus Christ, and thou shalt be saved" (Acts 16:31) is the message we have to deliver to you. If we address to you the longer form of the gospel, "He that believeth and is baptized shall be saved" (Mark 16:16), this is true of every living man, whatever his age may be. I am not afraid that this story of the dying and repenting thief, who went straight from the cross to the crown, will be used by you amiss. But if you are wicked enough so to use it, I cannot help it. I will only fulfill that solemn Scripture that declares that the gospel is a savor unto death to some, even that very gospel that is a savor of life unto life to others (2 Cor. 2:16).

But I do not think, dear friend, that the only speciality about the thief is the lateness of his repentance. So far from being the only point of interest, it is not even the chief point. To some minds, at any rate, other points will be even more remarkable. I want to show you very briefly that there was a speciality in his case as to *the means of his conversion.* Second, there was a speciality in *his faith.* Third, there was a speciality in *the result of his faith while he was there below.* And fourth, there was a speciality in *the promise won by his faith*—the promise fulfilled in him in Paradise.

## The Means by Which the Thief Was Converted

How do you think it was? Well, we do not know. We cannot tell. It seems to me that the man was an unconverted, impenitent thief when they nailed him to the cross, because one of the evangelists says, "The *thieves* also, which were crucified with him, cast the same in his teeth" (Matt. 27:44). I know that this may have been a general statement, and that it is reconcilable with its having been done by one thief only, according to the methods commonly used by critics. But I am not enamored of critics even when they are friendly. I have such respect for biblical revelation that I never in my own mind permit the idea of discrepancies and mistakes. When the evangelist says *they,* I believe he meant *they,* and that both these thieves did at their first crucifixion rail at the Christ with whom they were crucified. It would appear that by some means or other this thief must have been converted while he was on the cross. Assuredly nobody preached a sermon to him, no evangelistic address was delivered at the foot of his cross, and no meeting was held for special prayer on his account. He does not even seem to have had any instruction, or an invitation, or an expostulation addressed to him, and yet this man became a sincere and accepted believer in the Lord Jesus Christ.

Dwell upon this fact, if you please, and note its practical bearing upon the cases of many around us. There are many among my readers who have been instructed from their childhood, who have been admonished and warned and entreated and invited, and yet they have not come to Christ. Yet this man, without any of these advantages, nevertheless believed in the Lord Jesus Christ and found eternal life. O you who have lived under the sound of the gospel from your childhood, the thief does not comfort you, but he accuses you! What are you doing to abide so long in unbelief? Will you never believe the testimony of divine love? What more shall I say to you? What more can anyone say to you?

What do you think must have converted this poor thief? It strikes me that it must have been the sight of our great Lord and Savior. There was, to begin with, our Savior's wonderful behavior on the road to the cross. Perhaps the robber had mixed up with all sorts of society, but had never seen a man like this. Never had a cross been carried by a cross bearer of His look and fashion. The robber wondered who this meek and majestic person could be. He heard the women weep, and he wondered in himself whether any-body would ever weep for him. He thought that this must be some very singular person that the people should stand about Him with tears in their eyes. When he heard that mysterious Sufferer say so solemnly, "Daughters of Jerusalem, weep not for me, but weep for your children" (Luke 23:28), he must have been struck with won-der. When he came to think, in his death pangs, of the singular look of pity that Jesus cast on the women and of the self-forgetfulness that gleamed from His eyes, he was smitten with a strange relent-ing. It was as if an angel had crossed his path and opened his eyes to a new world and to a new form of manhood, the like of which he had never seen before. He and his companion were coarse, rough fellows. This was a delicately formed and fashioned being, of superior order to himself; yes, and of superior order to any other of the sons of men. Who could He be? What must He be? Though he could see that He suffered and fainted as He went along, he marked that there was no word of complaining, no note of con-demnation in return for the revilings cast upon Him. His eyes looked love on those who glared on Him with hate. Surely that march along the Via Dolorosa was the first part of the sermon that God preached to that bad man's heart. It was preached to many others who did not regard its teaching; but upon this man, by God's special grace, it had a softening effect when he came to think over it and consider it. Was it not a likely and convincing means of grace?

When he saw the Savior surrounded by the Roman soldiery—saw the executioners bring forth the hammers and the nails and lay Him down upon His back and drive the nails into His hands and feet—this crucified criminal was startled and astonished as he heard Him say, "Father, forgive them; for they know not what they do" (Luke 23:34). He himself probably had met his executioners with a curse, but he heard this man breathe a prayer to the great Father. And as a Jew, as he probably was, he understood what was meant by such a prayer. But it did astound him to hear Jesus pray for His murderers. That was a petition the like of which he had never heard or even dreamed. From whose lips could it come but from the lips of a divine being? Such a loving, forgiving, godlike prayer proved Him to be the Messiah. Who else had ever prayed so? Certainly not David and the kings of Israel, who, on the contrary, in all honesty and heartiness imprecated the wrath of God upon their enemies. Elijah himself would not have prayed in that fashion, but rather would have called fire from heaven on the centurion and his company. It was a new, strange sound to him. I do not suppose that he appreciated it to the full, but I can well believe that it deeply impressed him and made him feel that his fellow sufferer was a being about whom there was an exceeding mystery of goodness.

And when the cross was lifted up, that thief hanging up on his own cross looked around, and I suppose he could see that inscription written in three languages—"Jesus of Nazareth, the King of the Jews." If so, that writing was his little Bible, his New Testament, and he interpreted it by what he knew of the Old Testament. Putting this and that together—that strange person, incarnate loveliness, all patience and all majesty, that strange prayer, and now this singular inscription—surely he who knew the Old Testament, as I have no doubt he did, would say to himself, "Is this He? Is this truly the King of the Jews? This is He who wrought miracles and raised the dead and said that He was the Son of God. It is all true, and is He really our Messiah?"

Then he would remember the words of the prophet Isaiah: "He was despised and rejected of men; a man of sorrows, and acquainted with grief….Surely he hath borne our griefs, and carried our sorrows" (Isa. 53:3–4). "Why," he would say to himself, I never understood that passage before, but it must point to Him. The chastisement of our peace is upon Him. Can this be He who cried in the Psalms—"they pierced my hands and my feet" (22:16)? As he looked at Him again, he felt in his soul, "It must be Him. Could there be another so like to Him?" He felt conviction creeping over his spirit. Then he looked again, and he marked how all men down below rejected and despised and hissed and hooted Him, and all this would make the case the more clear. "All they that see me laugh me to scorn: they shoot out the lip, they shake the head, saying, He trusted on the LORD that he would deliver him: let him deliver him, seeing he delighted in him" (Ps. 22:7–8).

Perhaps this dying thief read the gospel out of the lips of Christ's enemies. They said, "He saved others." "Ah!" thought he, "did He save others? Why should He not save me?" What a grand bit of gospel that was for the dying thief—"He saved others"! "I think I could swim to heaven on that plank, because if He saved others, He can of a surety save me."

Thus the very things that the enemies disdainfully threw at Christ would be gospel to this poor dying man. When it has been my misery to read any of the wretched prints that are sent us out of scorn, in which our Lord is held up to ridicule, I have thought, "Why, perhaps those who read these loathsome blasphemies may, nevertheless, learn the gospel from them!" You may pick a jewel from dunghill and find its radiance undiminished. You may gather the gospel from a blasphemous mouth, and it shall be nonetheless the gospel of salvation. Perhaps this man learned the gospel from those who jested at our dying Lord, and so the servants of the devil were unconsciously made to be the servants of Christ.

But, after all, surely that which won him most must have been to look at Jesus again as He was hanging upon the cruel tree. Possibly nothing about the physical person of Christ would be attractive to him, for His visage was more marred than that of any man and His form more than the sons of men. But yet there must have been in that blessed face a singular charm. Was it not the very image of perfection? As I conceive the face of Christ, it was very different from anything that any painter has yet been able to place upon his canvas. It was all goodness and kindness and unselfishness, and yet it was a royal face. It was a face of superlative justice and unrivaled tenderness. Righteousness and uprightness sat upon His brow, but infinite pity and goodwill to men had also there taken up their abode. It was a face that would have struck you at once as one by itself, never to be forgotten, never to be fully understood. It was all sorrow, yet all love; all meekness, yet all resolution; all wisdom, yet all simplicity; the face of a child or an angel, and yet peculiarly the face of a man. Majesty and misery, suffering and sacredness, were therein strangely combined. He was evidently the Lamb of God, the Son of Man. As the robber looked, he believed. Is it not singular, the very sight of the Master won him? The sight of the Lord in agony and shame and death! Scarcely a word, certainly no sermon, no attending worship on the Sabbath, no reading of gracious books, no appeal from mother, or teacher, or friend, but the sight of Jesus won him. I put it down as a very singular thing, a thing for you and me to recollect and dwell upon with quite as much vividness as we do upon the lateness of this robber's conversion.

Oh, that God of His mercy might convert every reader! Oh, that I could have a share in it by declaring God's word! But I will be equally happy if you get to heaven anyhow. If the Lord should take you there without outward ministries, leading you to Jesus by some simple method such as He adopted with the thief, He shall have the glory of it, and His poor servant will be overjoyed! Oh, that you would now look to Jesus and live! Before your eyes He is set forth, evidently crucified among you. Look to Him and be saved, even at this hour.

## The Speciality of This Man's Faith

I greatly question whether the equal and the parallel of the dying thief's faith will be readily found outside the Scriptures or even in the Scriptures.

Observe, that this man believed in Christ *when he literally saw Him dying the death of a felon,* under circumstances of the greatest personal shame. You have never realized what it was to be crucified. None of you could do that, for the sight has never been seen in our day in England. There is not a man or woman here who has ever realized in his or her own mind the actual death of Christ. It stands beyond us. This man saw it with his own eyes, and for him to call *Him* "Lord" who was hanging on a gibbet was no small triumph of faith. For him to ask Jesus to remember him when He came into His kingdom, though he saw that Jesus bleeding His life away and hounded to the death, was a splendid act of reliance. For him to commit his everlasting destiny into the hands of One who was, to all appearance, unable even to preserve His own life was a noble achievement of faith. I say that this dying thief leads the way in the matter of faith, for what he saw of the circumstances of the Savior was calculated to contradict rather than help his confidence. What he saw was to his hindrance rather than to his help, for he saw our Lord in the very extremity of agony and death, and yet he believed in Him as the King shortly to come to His kingdom.

Recollect, too, that at that moment when the thief believed in

Christ, *all the disciples had forsaken Him and fled.* John might be lingering at a little distance, and holy women may have stood farther off, but no one was present to bravely champion the dying Christ. Judas had sold Him, Peter had denied Him, and the rest had forsaken Him; and it was then that the dying thief called Him "Lord" and said, "Remember me when thou comest into thy kingdom." I call that splendid faith. Why, some of you do not believe though you are surrounded with Christian friends and urged on by the testimony of those whom you regard with love. But this man, all alone, comes out and calls Jesus his Lord! No one else was confessing Christ at that moment. No revival was around Him with enthusiastic crowds. He was all by himself as a confessor of his Lord. After our Lord was nailed to the tree, the first to bear witness for Him was this thief. The centurion bore witness afterward, when our Lord expired; but this thief was a lone confessor, holding on to Christ when nobody would say "Amen" to what he said. Even his fellow thief was mocking at the crucified Savior, so that this man shone as a lone star in the midnight darkness. Oh, dare you be Daniels? Dare you stand alone? Would you dare to stand out amidst a ribald crew and say, "Jesus is my King. I only ask Him to remember me when He comes into His kingdom"? Would you be likely to avow such a faith when priests and scribes, princes and people, were all mocking at the Christ and deriding Him? Brethren, the dying robber exhibited marvelous faith, and I beg you to think of this next time you speak of him.

And it seems to me that another point adds splendor to that faith, namely, that *he himself was in extreme torture.* Remember, he was crucified. It was a crucified man trusting in a crucified Christ. Oh, when our frame is racked with torture, when the tenderest nerves are pained, when our body is hung up to die by we know not what great length of torment, then to forget the present and live in the future is a grand achievement of faith! While dying, to turn your eye to another dying at your side and trust your soul with Him is very marvelous faith. Blessed thief, because they put you down at the bottom, as one of the least of saints, I think that I must bid you come up higher and take one of the uppermost seats among those who by faith have glorified the Christ of God!

Why, see, dear friend, once more, the speciality of this man's faith was that *he saw so much,* though his eyes had been opened for so short a time! He saw the future world. He was not a believer in annihilation or in the possibility of a man's not being immortal. The thief evidently expected to be in another world and to be in existence when the dying Lord should come into His kingdom. He believed all that, and it is more than some do nowadays. He also believed that Jesus would have a kingdom, a kingdom after He was dead, a kingdom though He was crucified. He believed that Jesus was winning for Himself a kingdom by those nailed hands and pierced feet. This was intelligent faith, was it not? The thief believed that Jesus would have a kingdom in which others would share, and therefore he aspired to have his portion in it. Yet he had fit views of himself, and therefore he did not say, "Lord, let me sit at your right hand" or "Let me share of the dainties of your palace." But he said only, "Remember me. Think of me. Cast an eye my way. Think of Your poor dying comrade on the cross at Your right hand. Lord, remember me. Remember me." I see deep humility in the prayer and yet a sweet, joyous, confident exaltation of the Christ at the time when the Christ was in His deepest humiliation.

If you have thought of this dying thief only as one who put off repentance, I want you now to believe of him as one that did greatly and grandly believe in Christ. And oh, that you would do the same! Oh, that you would put a great confidence in my great Lord! Never did a poor sinner trust Christ too much. There was never a case of a guilty one who believed that Jesus could forgive him and afterward found that He could not—who believed that Jesus could save him on the spot and then woke up to find that it was a delusion. No; plunge into this river of confidence in Christ. The waters are waters to swim in, not to drown in. Never did a soul perish that glorified Christ by a living, loving faith in Him. Come, then, with all your sin, whatever it may be, with all your deep depression of spirits, all your agony of conscience. Come and grasp my Lord and Master with both the hands of your faith, and He shall be yours, and you shall be His.

*Turn to Christ your longing eyes,*
*View His bloody sacrifice:*
*See in Him your sins forgiven;*
*Pardon, holiness, and heaven;*
*Glorify the King of kings,*
*Take the peace the gospel brings.*

## The Result of His Faith

I have heard people say, "Well, you see, the dying thief was converted. But then he was not baptized. He never went to communion and never joined the church." He could not do either, and that which God Himself renders impossible to us He does not demand of us. The thief was nailed to the cross; how could he be baptized? But he did a great deal more than that; for if he could not carry out the outward signs, he most manifestly exhibited the things that they signified, which, in his condition, was better still.

*This dying thief first of all confessed the Lord Jesus Christ,* and that is the very essence of baptism. He confessed Christ. Did he not acknowledge Him to his fellow thief? It was as open a confession as he could make it. Did he not acknowledge Christ before all who were gathered around the cross who were within hearing? It was as public a confession as he could possibly cause it to be. Yet certain cowardly fellows claim to be Christians, though they have never confessed Christ to a single person, and then they quote this poor thief as an excuse. Are they nailed to a cross? Are they dying in agony? Oh, no; and yet they talk as if they could claim the exemption that these circumstances would give them. What a dishonest piece of business!

The fact is that our Lord requires an open confession as well as a secret faith. And if you will not render it, there is no promise of salvation for you but a threat of being denied in the last. The apostle puts it: "If thou shalt confess with thy mouth the Lord Jesus, and shalt believe in thine heart that God hath raised him from the dead, thou shalt be saved" (Rom. 10:9). It is stated in another place, "He that believeth and is baptized shall be saved" (Mark 16:16). That is Christ's way of making the confession of Him. If there be a true faith, there must be a declaration of it. If you are candles and God has lit you, "Let your light so shine before men, that they may see your good works, and glorify your Father which is in heaven" (Matt. 5:16). Soldiers of Christ must, like Her Majesty's soldiers, wear their uniforms. If they are ashamed of their uniforms, they should be drummed out of the regiment. They are not honest soldiers who refuse to march in rank with their comrades. The very least thing that the Lord Jesus Christ can expect of us is that we do confess Him to the best of our power. If you are nailed up to a cross, I will not invite you to be baptized. If you are fastened to a tree to die, I will not ask you to come into this pulpit and declare your faith, for you cannot. But you are required to do what you can do, namely, to make as distinct and open an avowal of the Lord Jesus Christ as may be suitable in your present condition.

I believe that many Christian people get into a great deal of trouble through not being honest in their convictions. For instance, if a man goes into a workplace or a soldier into a barracks room, and if he does not fly his flag from the first, it will be very difficult for him to run it up afterward. But if he immediately and boldly lets them know, "I am a Christian, and there are certain things that I cannot help doing, though they displease you"—when that is clearly understood, after a while the singularity of the thing will be gone, and the man will be let alone. But if he is a little sneaky and thinks that he is going to please the world and please Christ, too he is in for a rough time, let him depend upon it. His life will be that of a fox in a dog kennel if he tries the way of compromise. That will never do. Come out. Show your colors. Let it be known who you are and what you are. And although your course will not be smooth, it will certainly be not half so rough as if you tried to run with the hare and hunt with the hounds—a very difficult piece of business that. This man came out, then and there, and made as open an avowal of his faith in Christ as was possible.

*The next thing he did was to rebuke his fellow sinner.* He spoke it to him in answer to the ribaldry with which he had assailed our Lord. I do not know what the unconverted convict had been blasphemously saying, but his converted comrade spoke very honestly to him. "Dost not thou fear God, seeing thou art in the same condemnation? And we indeed justly; for we receive the due reward of our deeds: but this man hath done nothing amiss." It is more than ever needful in these days that believers in Christ should not allow sin to go unrebuked, and yet a great many of them do so. Do you not know that a person who is silent when a wrong thing is said or done may become a participator in the sin? If you do not rebuke sin—I mean, of course, on all fit occasions and in a proper spirit—your silence will give consent to the sin, and you will be an aider and abettor in it. A man who saw a robbery and who did not cry, "Stop, thief!" would be thought to be in league with the thief. The man who can hear swearing or see impurity and never utter a word of protest may well question whether he is right himself. Our "other men's sins" make up a great item in our personal guilt unless we in anyway rebuke them. This our Lord expects us to do. The dying thief did it, and did it with all his heart, and therein far exceeded large numbers of those who hold their heads high in the church.

Next, *the dying thief made a full confession of his guilt.* He said to him who was hanged with him, "Dost not thou fear God, seeing thou art in the same condemnation? *And we indeed justly.*" Not many words, but what a world of meaning was in them—"we indeed justly." "You and I are dying for our crimes," said he, "and we deserve to die." When a man is willing to confess that he deserves the wrath of God—that he deserves the suffering that his sin has brought upon him—there is evidence of sincerity in him. In this man's case, his repentance glittered like a holy tear in the eye of his faith, so that his faith was bejeweled with the drops of His penitence. As I have often said, I suspect the faith that is not born as a twin with repentance. But there is no room for suspicion in the case of this penitent confessor. I pray God that you and I may have such a thorough work as this in our own hearts as the result of our faith.

Then, see, *this dying thief defends his Lord right manfully.* He says, "We indeed justly, but this man hath done nothing amiss." Was not that beautifully said? He did not say, "This man does not deserve to die," but said, "This man hath done nothing amiss." He means that Jesus is perfectly innocent. He does not even say, "He has done nothing wicked," but he even asserts that He has not acted unwisely or indiscreetly—"This Man hath done nothing amiss." This is a glorious testimony of a dying man to One who was numbered with the transgressors and was being put to death because His enemies falsely accused Him. Beloved, I only pray that you and I may bear as good witness to our Lord as this thief did. He outruns us all. We need not think much of the coming of his conversion late in life. We may far rather consider how blessed was the testimony that he bore for his Lord when it was most needed. When all other voices were silent, one suffering penitent spoke out and said, "This man hath done nothing amiss."

See, again, another mark of this man's faith. He prays, and *his prayer is directed to Jesus.* "Lord, remember me when thou comest into thy kingdom." True faith is always praying faith. "Behold, he prayeth," is one of the surest tests of the new birth. O friends, may we abound in prayer, for thus we shall prove that our faith in Jesus

Christ is what it should be! This converted robber opened his mouth wide in prayer. He prayed with great confidence as to the coming kingdom, and he sought that kingdom first, even to the exclusion of all else. He might have asked for life or for ease from pain, but he prefers the kingdom, and this is a high mark of grace.

In addition to thus praying, you will see that *he adores and worships Jesus,* for he says, "Lord, remember me when thou comest into thy kingdom." The petition is worded as if he felt, "Only let Christ think of me, and it is enough. Let Him but remember me, and the thought of His mind will be effectual for everything that I shall need in the world to come." This is to impute Godhead to Christ. If a man can cast his all upon the mere memory of a person to be remembered by the Lord Jesus is all that this man asks or desires, he pays to the Lord great honor. I think that there was about his prayer a worship equal to the eternal hallelujahs of cherubim and seraphim. There was in it a glorification of his Lord that is not exceeded even by the endless symphonies of angelic spirits who surround the throne. Thief, you have done well!

Oh, that some penitent spirit might be helped thus to believe, thus to confess, thus to defend his Master, thus to adore, thus to worship; and then the age of the convert would be a matter of the smallest imaginable consequence.

## Our Lord's Word to Him About the World to Come

He said to the thief, "Today shalt thou be with me in paradise." He only asked the Lord to remember him, but he obtained this surprising answer, "Today shalt thou be with me in paradise."

In some respects I envy this dying thief, for this reason—that when the Lord pardoned most of us He did not give us a place in paradise that same day. We are not yet come to the rest that is promised to us. No, you are waiting here. Some of you have been waiting very long. It is thirty years with many of us. It is forty years, it is fifty years, with many others since the Lord blotted out your sins, and yet you are not with Him in paradise. There is a dear member of this church who, I suppose, has known the Lord for seventy-five years, and she is still with us, having long passed her ninetieth year. The Lord did not admit her to paradise on the day of her conversion. He did not take any one of us from nature to grace, and from grace to glory, in a day. We have had to wait a good while. There is something for us to do in the wilderness, and so we are kept out of the heavenly garden. This robber breakfasted with the devil, but he dined with Christ on earth and supped with Him in paradise. This was short work but blessed work. What a host of troubles he escaped! What a world of temptation he missed! What an evil world he quitted! He was just born, like a lamb dropped in the field, and then he was lifted into the Shepherd's bosom straightaway. I do not remember the Lord ever saying this to anybody else. I dare say it may have happened that souls have been converted and have gone home at once, but I never heard of anybody who had such an assurance from Christ as this man had. "Verily, I say unto thee"—such a personal assurance: "Verily I say unto *thee*, To day shalt thou be with me in paradise" (Luke 23:43). Dying thief, you were favored above many, "to be with Christ; which is far better" (Phil. 1:23), and to be with Him so soon!

Why is it that our Lord does not thus emparadise all of us at once? It is because there is something for us to do on earth. My brethren, are you still doing it? *Are you doing it?* Some good people are still on earth, but why? What is the use of them? I cannot make it out. If they are indeed the Lord's people, what are they here for? They get up in the morning and eat their breakfast, and in due course eat their dinner, and their supper, and go to bed and sleep. At the proper hour they get up the next morning and do the same as on the previous day. Is this living for Jesus? Is this life? It does not come to much. Can this be the life of God in man? O Christian people, do justify your Lord in keeping you waiting here! How can you justify Him but by serving Him to the utmost of your power? The Lord help you to do so? Why, you owe as much to Him as the dying thief! I know I owe a great deal more. What a mercy it is to have been converted while you were yet a boy, to be brought to the Savior while you were yet a girl! What a debt of obligation young Christians owe to the Lord! And if this poor thief crammed a life full of testimony into a few minutes, ought not you and I, who are spared, for years after conversion perform good service for our Lord? Come, let us wake up if we have been asleep! Let us begin to live if we have been half dead. May the Spirit of God make something of us yet, so that we may go as industrious servants from the labors of the vineyard to the pleasures of the paradise! To our once crucified Lord be glory forever and ever! Amen.

*D*oes it not appear as if the death that that darkness shrouded was also a natural part of the great whole? We have grown at last to feel as if the death of the Christ of God were an integral part of human history. You cannot take it out of man's chronicle, can you? Introduce the Fall and see Paradise Lost, and you cannot make the poem complete till you have introduced that greater Man who did redeem us and by His death gave us our Paradise Regained. It is a singular characteristic of all true miracles that though your wonder never ceases, they never appear to be unnatural. They are marvelous but never monstrous. The miracles of Christ dovetail into the general run of human history. We cannot see how the Lord could be on earth and Lazarus not be raised from the dead when the grief of Martha and Mary had told its tale. We cannot see how the disciples could have been tempest-tossed on the Lake of Galilee and the Christ not walk on the water to deliver them. Wonders of power are expected parts of the narrative where Jesus is. Everything fits into its place with surrounding facts. But the miracles of Jesus, this of the darkness among them, are essential to human history. And especially is this so in the case of His death and this great darkness that shrouded it. All things in human story converge to the cross which seems to be not an afterthought or an expedient but the fit and foreordained channel through which love should run to guilty men.

# Chapter Six

# The Three
# Hours' Darkness

*Now from the sixth hour there was darkness over all the land
unto the ninth hour*—Matthew 27:45.

FROM NINE TILL NOON the usual degree
of light was present, so that there was time enough for our Lord's
adversaries to behold and insult His sufferings. There could be no
mistake about the fact that He was really nailed to the cross, for He
was crucified in broad daylight. We are fully assured that it was
Jesus of Nazareth, for both friends and foes were eyewitnesses of
His agonies. For three long hours the Jews sat down and watched
Him on the cross, making jests of His miseries. I feel thankful for
those three hours of light. Otherwise, the enemies of our faith
would have questioned whether in very deed the blessed body of
our Master was nailed to the tree and would have started rumors
as many as the bats and owls that haunt the darkness. Where
would have been the witnesses of this solemn scene if the sun had
been hidden from morn till night? As three hours of light gave
opportunity for inspection and witness bearing, we see the wisdom
did not allow it to close too soon.

Never forget that this miracle of the darkness at high noon was
performed by our Lord in His weakness. He had walked the sea,
raised the dead, and healed the sick in the days of His strength. But
now He has come to His lowest, the fever is on Him, He is faint and

thirsty. He hangs on the borders of death, yet has He power to darken the sun at noon. He is still very God of very God:

> *Behold, a purple torrent run*
> *Down from His hands and head,*
> *The crimson tide puts out the sun;*
> *His groans awake the dead.*

If He can do this in His weakness, what is He not able to do in His strength? Do not fail to remember that this power was displayed in a sphere in which He did not usually put forth His might. The sphere of Christ is that of goodness and benevolence, and consequently of light. When He enters the sphere of darkness making and of working judgment, He engages in what He calls His strange work. Wonders of terror are His left-handed deeds. It is but now and then that He causes the sun to go down at noon and darkens the earth in the clear day (Amos 8:9). If our Lord can make darkness at will as He dies, what glory may we not expect now that He lives to be the light of the city of God forever? The Lamb is the light, and what a light! The heavens bear the mark of His dying power and lose their brightness. Shall not the new heavens and the new earth attest to the power of the risen Lord? The thick darkness around the dying Christ is the robe of the Omnipotent. He lives again, all power is in His hands, and all that power He will put forth to bless His chosen.

What a call must that midday midnight have been to the careless sons of men! They did not know that the Son of God was among them or that He was working out human redemption. The grandest hour in all history seemed likely to pass by unheeded, when suddenly, night hastened from her chambers and usurped the day. Everyone asked his fellow, "What means this darkness?" Business stood still, the plow stayed in mid-furrow, and the axe paused uplifted. It was the midday, when men are busiest, but they made a general pause. Not only on Calvary, but also on every hill and in every valley, the gloom settled down. There was a halt in the caravan of life. None could move unless they groped their way like the blind. The master of the house called for a light at noon, and his servant tremblingly obeyed the unusual summons. Other lights were twinkling, and Jerusalem was a city by night, only men were not in their beds.

How startled was mankind! Around the great deathbed an appropriate quiet was secured. I doubt not that a shuddering awe came over the masses of the people and the thoughtful foresaw terrible things. Those who had stood around the cross and insulted the majesty of Jesus were paralyzed with fear. They ceased their ribaldry and with it their cruel exultation. They were cowed though not convinced, even the basest of them, while the better sort "smote their breasts, and returned" (Luke 23:48). As many as could do so, no doubt, stumbled to their homes and endeavored to hide themselves for fear of awful judgments that they feared were near.

I do not wonder that there should be traditions of strange things that were said during the hush of that darkness. Those whispers of the past may or may not be true, and they have been the subject of learned controversy, but the labor of the dispute was energy ill spent. Yet we could not have wondered if one did say as he is reported to have done, "God is suffering, or the world is perishing." Nor should I drive from my beliefs the poetic legend that an Egyptian pilot passing down the river heard among the reedy banks a voice out of the rustling rushes, whispering, "The great Pan is dead." Truly, the God of nature was expiring, and things less tender than the reeds by the river might well tremble at the sound thereof.

We are told that this darkness was over all the land. Luke says it was "over all the earth" (Luke 23:44). That portion of our globe that was then veiled in natural night was not affected, but to all men who were awake and at their employment, it was the advertisement of a great and solemn event. It was strange beyond all experience, and all men marveled, for when the light should have been brightest, all things were obscured for the space of three hours.

There must be great teaching in this darkness, for when we come so near the cross, which is the center of history, every event is full of meaning. Light will come out of this darkness. I love to feel the solemnity of the three hours of death-shade and to sit down therein and meditate, with no companion but the august Sufferer, around whom that darkness lowered. I am going to write of it in four ways, as the Holy Spirit may help me. First, let us bow our spirits in the presence of *a miracle that amazes us.* Second, let us regard this darkness as *a veil that conceals.* Third, let us regard this darkness as *a symbol that instructs.* And fourth, let us regard this

darkness as *a display of sympathy* that forewarns us by the prophecies that it implies.

## A Miracle That Amazes Us

It may seem a trite observation that this darkness was altogether out of the natural course of things. Since the world began, it
was not heard of that at high noon there should be darkness over
all the land. It was out of the order of nature altogether. Some people deny miracles; and if they also deny God, I will not at this time
deal with them. But it is very strange that anyone who believes in
God should doubt the possibility of miracles. It seems to me that,
granted the being of a God, miracles are to be expected as occa-
sional declarations of His independent and active will. He may
make certain rules for His actions, and it may be His wisdom to
keep to them. But surely He must reserve to Himself the liberty to
depart from His own laws, or else He has in a measure laid aside
His personal Godhead, deified law, and set it up above Himself. It
would not increase our idea of the glory of His Godhead if we
could be assured that He had made Himself subject to rule and tied
His own hands from ever acting except in a certain manner. From
the self-existence and freedom of will that enter into our very conception of God, we are led to expect that sometimes He should not
keep to the methods that He follows as His general rule. This has
led to the universal conviction that a miracle is a proof of Godhead.
The general works of creation and providence are to my mind the
best proofs. But the common heart of our race, for some reason or
other, looks to miracles as surer evidence, thus proving that miracles are expected of God.

Although the Lord makes it His order that there shall be day
and night, He in this case with abundant reason interposes three
hours of night in the center of a day. Behold the reason. The
unusual in lower nature is made to consort with the unusual in the
dealings of nature's Lord. Certainly this miracle was most congru-
ous with that greater miracle that was happening in the death of
Christ. Was not the Lord Himself departing from all common
ways? Was He not doing that which had never been done from the
beginning and would never be done again? That man should die is
so common a thing as to be deemed inevitable. We are not startled
now at the sound of a funeral knell. As the companions of our
youth die at our side, we are not seized with amazement, for death

is everywhere about us and within us. But that the Son of God should die, this is beyond all expectation, and not only above nature but also contrary thereto. He who is equal with God deigns to hang upon the cross and die. I know of nothing that seems more out of rule and beyond expectation than this. The sun darkened at noon is a fit accompaniment of the death of Jesus. Is it not so?

Further, this miracle was not only out of the order of nature, but it was one that *would have been pronounced impossible*. It is not possible that there should be an eclipse of the sun at the time of the full moon. The moon at the time when she is in her full is not in a position in which she could possibly cast her shadow upon the earth. The Passover was at the time of the full moon, and therefore it was not possible that the sun should then undergo an eclipse. This darkening of the sun was not strictly an astronomical eclipse. The darkness was doubtless produced in some other way, yet to those who were present, it did seem to be a total eclipse of the sun—a thing impossible. Ah, when we come to deal with man, and the fall, and sin, and God, and Christ, and the atonement, we are at home with impossibilities. We have now reached a region where prodigies and marvels and surprises are the order of the day. Sublimities become commonplaces when we come within the circle of eternal love. Yes, and even more. We have now quitted the solid land of the possible and have put out to sea, where we see the works of the Lord and His wonders in the deep. The way of the cross is ablaze with the divine, and we soon perceive that "with God all things are possible" (Matt. 19:26). See, then, in the death of Jesus, the possibility of the impossible! Behold how the Son of God can die. We sometimes pause when we meet with an expression in a hymn that implies that God can suffer or die. We think that the poet has used too great a license, yet it behooves us to refrain from hypercriticism, since in Holy Writ there are words like it. We even read (Acts 20:28) of "the church of God, which he hath purchased with his own blood"—the blood of God! Ah, well! I am not careful to defend the language of the Holy Ghost, but in its presence, I take liberty to justify the words of the hymn just now:

> *Well might the sun in darkness hide,*
> *And shut his glories in,*
> *When God, the mighty Maker, died*
> *For man, the creature's sin.*

I will not venture to explain the death of the incarnate God. I am content to believe it and to rest my hope upon it.

How should the Holy One have sin laid upon Him? That also I do not know. A wise man has told us, as if it were an axiom, that the imputation or the nonimputation of sin is an impossibility. Be it so: We have become familiar with such things since we have beheld the cross. Things that men call absurdities have become foundation truths to us. The doctrine of the cross is to them that perish foolishness. We do know that in our Lord was no sin, and yet He bare our sins in His body on the tree. We do not know how the innocent Son of God could be permitted to suffer for sins that were not His own. It amazes us that justice should permit one so perfectly holy to be forsaken of His God and to cry out, "Eloi, Eloi, lama sabachthani?" But it was so, and we rejoice therein. As the sun was eclipsed when it was impossible that it should be eclipsed, so has Jesus performed on our behalf, in the agonies of His death, things that in the ordinary judgment of men must be set down as utterly impossible. Our faith is at home in wonderland, where the Lord's thoughts are seen to be as high above our thoughts as the heavens are above the earth.

Concerning this miracle, I have also further to remark that *this darkening of the sun surpassed all ordinary and natural eclipses*. It lasted longer than an ordinary eclipse, and it came in a different manner. According to Luke, the darkness all over the land came first, and the sun was darkened afterward. The darkness did not begin with the sun, but it mastered the sun. It was unique and supernatural. Now, among all griefs, no grief is comparable to the grief of Jesus, and of all woes, none can parallel the woes of our great Substitute. As strongest light casts deepest shade, so has the surprising love of Jesus cost Him a death such as falls not to the common lot of men. Others die, but this Man is "obedient unto death" (Phil. 2:8). Others drink the fatal draught, yet care not of its wormwood and gall, but He "should taste death" (Heb. 2:9). "He hath poured out his soul unto death" (Isa. 53:12). Every part of His being was darkened with that extraordinary death-shade, and the natural darkness outside of Him did but shroud a special death that was entirely by itself.

And now, when I come to think of it, *this darkness appears to have been most natural and fitting*. If we had to write out the story of our Lord's death, we could not omit the darkness without neglecting a most important item. The darkness seems a part of the natural furniture of that great transaction. Read the story through and you are not at all startled with the darkness. After once familiarizing your mind with the thought that this is the Son of God who stretches His hands to the cruel death of the cross, you do not wonder at the rending of the veil of the temple. You are not astonished at the earthquake or at the rising of certain of the dead. These are proper attendants of our Lord's passion, and so is the darkness. It seems as if it could not have been otherwise.

For a moment think again. Does it not appear as if the death that that darkness shrouded was also a natural part of the great whole? We have grown at last to feel as if the death of the Christ of God were an integral part of human history. You cannot take it out of man's chronicle, can you? Introduce the Fall and see Paradise Lost, and you cannot make the poem complete till you have introduced that greater Man who did redeem us and by His death gave us our Paradise Regained. It is a singular characteristic of all true miracles that though your wonder never ceases, they never appear to be unnatural. They are marvelous but never monstrous. The miracles of Christ dovetail into the general run of human history. We cannot see how the Lord could be on earth and Lazarus not be raised from the dead when the grief of Martha and Mary had told its tale. We cannot see how the disciples could have been tempest-tossed on the Lake of Galilee and the Christ not walk on the water to deliver them. Wonders of power are expected parts of the narrative where Jesus is. Everything fits into its place with surrounding facts. But the miracles of Jesus, this of the darkness among them, are essential to human history. And especially is this so in the case of His death and this great darkness that shrouded it. All things in human story converge to the cross which seems to be not an afterthought or an expedient but the fit and foreordained channel through which love should run to guilty men.

Sit down and let the thick darkness cover you till you cannot even see the cross, and only know that out of reach of mortal eye your Lord wrought out the redemption of His people. He wrought in silence a miracle of patience and of love, by which light has come to those who sit in darkness and in the valley of the shadow of death.

## A Veil That Conceals

The Christ is hanging on yonder tree. I see the dreadful cross. I can see the thieves on either side. I look around, and I sorrowfully mark that motley group of citizens from Jerusalem, and scribes and priests and strangers from different countries, mingled with Roman soldiers. They turn their eyes on Him and for the most part gaze with cruel scorn upon the Holy One who is in the center. In truth it is an awful sight. Mark those dogs of the common sort and those bulls of Bashan of more notable rank who all unite to dishonor the meek and lowly One. I must confess I never read the story of the Master's death, knowing what I do of the pain of crucifixion, without deep anguish. Crucifixion was a death worthy to have been invented by devils. The pain that it involved was immeasurable, and I will not torture you by describing it. I know dear hearts that cannot read of it without tears and without lying awake for nights afterward.

But there was more than anguish upon Calvary: Ridicule and contempt embittered all. Those jests, those cruel gibes, those mockeries, those thrustings out of the tongue, what shall we say of these? The pain of the victim was grievous enough, but the abominable wickedness of the mockers who could bear? Let us thank God that in the middle of the crime there came down a darkness that rendered it impossible for them to go further with it. Jesus must die. For His pains there must be no alleviation, and from death there must be for Him no deliverance. But the scoffers must be silenced. Most effectually their mouths were closed by the dense darkness that shut them in.

What I see in that veil is, first of all, that it was *a concealment for those guilty enemies*. Did you ever think of that? It is as if God Himself said, "I cannot bear it. I will not see this infamy! Descend, O veil!" Down fell the heavy shades.

> *I asked the heavens, What foe to God hath done*
> *This unexampled deed? The heavens exclaim,*
> *Twas man; and we in horror snatched the sun*
> *From such a spectacle of guilt and shame.*

Thank God the cross is a hiding place. It furnishes for guilty men a shelter from the all-seeing eye so that justice need not see and strike. When God lifts up His Son and makes Him visible, He hides the sin of men. He says that "the times of this ignorance God winked at" (Acts 17:30). Even the greatness of their sin He casts behind His back, so that He need not see it but may indulge His long-suffering, permitting His pity to endure their provocations. It must have grieved the heart of the eternal God to see such wanton cruelty of men toward Him who went about doing good and healing all manner of diseases. It was horrible to see the teachers of the people rejecting Him with scorn, the seed of Israel, who should have accepted Him as their Messiah, casting Him out as a thing despised and abhorred. I therefore feel gratitude to God for bidding that darkness cover all the land and end that shameful scene. I would say to any guilty one, thank God that the Lord Jesus has made it possible for your sins to be hidden more completely than by thick darkness. Thank God that in Christ He does not see you with that stern eye of justice that would involve your destruction. Had not Jesus interposed, whose death you have despised, you had wrought out in your own death the result of your own sin long ago. But for your Lord's sake you are allowed to live as if God did not see you. This long-suffering is meant to bring you to repentance. Will you not come?

But, further, that darkness was *a sacred concealment for the blessed Person of our divine Lord.* So to speak, the angels found for their King a pavilion of thick clouds, in which His Majesty might be sheltered in its hour of misery. It was too much for wicked eyes to gaze so rudely on that immaculate Person. Had not His enemies stripped Him naked and cast lots for His robe? Therefore, it was right that the holy manhood should at length find suitable concealment. It was not fit that brutal eyes should see the lines made upon that blessed form by the graving tool of sorrow. It was not proper that revelers should see the contortions of that sacred frame, indwelt with Deity, while He was being broken beneath the iron rod of divine wrath on our behalf. It was right that God should cover Him so that none should see all He did and all He bare when He was made sin for us. I bless God devoutly for thus hiding my Lord away. Thus was He screened from eyes that were not fit to see the sun much less to look upon the Sun of Righteousness.

This darkness also warns us, even those of us who are the most reverent. This darkness tells us all that *the Passion is a great mystery into which we cannot pry.* I try to explain it as substitution, and I feel that where the language of Scripture is explicit, I may and must be explicit, too. But yet I feel that the idea of substitution does not cover the whole of the matter and that no human conception can completely grasp the whole of the dread mystery. It was wrought in darkness because the full, far-reaching meaning and result cannot be beheld of finite mind. Tell me the death of the Lord Jesus was a grand example of self-sacrifice—I can see *that* and much more. Tell me it was a wondrous obedience to the will of God—I can see *that* and much more. Tell me it was the bearing of what should have been borne by myriads of sinners of the human race, as the chastisement of their sin—I can see *that*, and found my best hope upon it. But do not tell me that this is all that is in the cross. No, great as this would be, there is much more in our Redeemer's death. God only knows the love of God. Christ only knows all that He accomplished when He bowed His head and gave up the ghost. There are common mysteries of nature into which it is irreverent to pry, but this is a divine mystery before which we put our shoes from off our feet, for the place called Calvary is holy ground. God veiled the cross in darkness, and in darkness much of its deeper meaning lies—not because God would not reveal it but because we do not have enough capacity to discern it all. God was manifest in the flesh, and in that human flesh He put away sin by His own sacrifice. This we all know, but "without controversy great is the mystery of godliness" (1 Tim. 3:16).

Once again, this veil of darkness also pictures to me the way in which *the powers of darkness will always endeavor to conceal the cross of Christ*. We fight with darkness when we try to preach the cross. "This is your hour, and the power of darkness," said Christ (Luke 22:53). I doubt not that the infernal hosts made in that hour a fierce assault upon the spirit of our Lord. This much also we know, that if the prince of darkness be anywhere in force, it is sure to be where Christ is lifted up. To cover the cross is the grand object of the enemy of souls. Did you ever notice it? These fellows who hate the gospel will let every other doctrine pass by, but if the atonement be preached and the truths that grow out of it, they are aroused immediately. Nothing provides the devil like the cross. Modern theology has for its main object the obscuration of the doctrine of atonement. It makes out sin to be a trifle and the punishment of it to be a temporary business, thus degrading the remedy by underrating the disease. We are not ignorant of its devices. Expect that the clouds of darkness will gather as to a center around the cross, but that they may hide it from the sinner's view. But expect this also, that the enemy's darkness shall meet its end. Light springs out of that darkness—the light eternal of the undying Son of God, who having risen from the dead lives forever to scatter the darkness of evil.

## A Symbol That Instructs

The veil falls down and conceals, but at the same time, as an emblem, it reveals. It seems to say, "Attempt not to search within, but learn from the veil itself: It hath cherub work upon it." This darkness teaches us what Jesus suffered. It aids us to guess at the griefs that we may not actually see.

The darkness is the symbol of *the wrath of God that fell on those who slew His only begotten Son.* God was angry, and His frown removed the light of day. Well might He be angry, when sin was murdering His only Son. The Jewish husbandmen were saying, "This is the heir; come, let us kill him, and let us seize on his inheritance" (Matt. 21:38). This is God's wrath toward all mankind, for practically all men concurred in the death of Jesus. That wrath has brought men into a darkness whereby they are ignorant, blinded, bewildered. They have come to love darkness rather than light because their deeds are evil (John 3:19). In that darkness they do not repent but go on to reject the Christ of God. Into this darkness God cannot look upon them in complacency. He views them as children of darkness and heirs of wrath, for whom is reserved the blackness of darkness forever.

The symbol also tells us *what our Lord Jesus Christ endured.* The darkness outside of Him was the figure of the darkness that was within Him. In Gethsemane a thick darkness fell upon our Lord's spirit. He was "exceeding sorrowful, even unto death" (Matt. 26:38). His joy was communion with God—that joy was gone, and He was in the dark. His day was the light of His Father's face: That face was hidden and a terrible night gathered around Him. I should sin against that veil if I were to pretend that I could tell you what the sorrow was that oppressed the Savior's soul. Have you ever felt a deep and overwhelming horror of sin—your own sin and the sins of others? Have you ever seen sin in the light of God's love? Has it ever darkly hovered over your sensitive conscience? Has an unknown sense of wrath crept over you like midnight gloom, and has it been about you, around you, above you, and within you? Have you felt shut up in your feebleness and yet shut out from God? Have you looked around and found no help, no comfort even in God—no hope, no peace? In all this you have sipped a little of that salt sea into which our Lord was cast. If, like Abraham, you have felt a horror of great darkness creep over you, then have you had a taste of what your divine Lord suffered when it pleased the Father to bruise Him and to put Him to grief.

This it was that made Him sweat great drops of blood falling to the ground, and this it was that on the cross made Him utter that appalling cry, "My God, my God, why hast thou forsaken me?" It was not the crown of thorns, or the scourge, or the cross that made Him cry, but the darkness, the awful darkness of desertion that oppressed His mind and made Him feel like one distraught. All that could comfort Him was withdrawn, and all that could distress Him was piled upon Him. "The spirit of a man will sustain his infirmity; but a wounded spirit who can bear?" (Prov. 18:14). Our Savior's spirit was wounded, and He cried, "My heart is like wax; it is melted in the midst of my bowels" (Ps. 22:14). Of all natural and spiritual comfort He was bereft, and His distress was utter and entire. The darkness of Calvary did not, like an ordinary night, reveal the stars, but it darkened every lamp of heaven. His strong crying and tears denoted the deep sorrow of His soul. He bore all it was possible for His capacious mind to bear, though enlarged and invigorated by union with the Godhead. He bore the equivalent of hell; nay, not that only but He bore that which stood instead of ten thousand hells so far as the vindication of the law is concerned. Our Lord rendered in His death agony a homage to justice far greater than if a world had been doomed to destruction. When I have said that, what more can I say? Well may I tell you that this unutterable darkness, this hiding of the divine face, expresses more of the woes of Jesus than words can ever tell.

I also see in the darkness *what it was that Jesus was battling with*, for we must never forget that the cross was a battlefield to Him, wherein He triumphed gloriously. He was fighting then with darkness, with the powers of darkness of which Satan is the head, and with the darkness of human ignorance, depravity, and falsehood. The battle thus apparent at Golgotha has been raging ever since. Then was the conflict at its height, for the chiefs of the two great armies met in personal conflict. The present battle in which you and I take our little share is as nothing compared with that wherein all the powers of darkness in their dense battalions hurled themselves against the Almighty Son of God. He bore their onset, endured the tremendous shock of their assault, and in the end, with shout of victory, He led captivity captive. He by His power and Godhead turned midnight into day again and brought back to this world a reign of light that shall never come to a close. Come to battle again, ye hosts of darkness, if ye dare! The cross has defeated you, and the cross shall defeat you. Hallelujah! The cross is the ensign of victory. Its light is the death of darkness. The cross is the lighthouse that guides poor weatherbeaten humanity into the harbor of peace. This is the lamp that shines over the door of the great Father's house to lead His prodigals home. Let us not be afraid of all the darkness that besets us on our way home, since Jesus is the Light that conquers it all.

The darkness never came to an end till the Lord Jesus broke the silence. All had been still, and the darkness had grown terrible. At last He spoke, and His voice uttered a psalm. It was the twenty-second psalm, "My God," saith He, "my God, why hast thou forsaken me?" Each repeated "Eloi" flashed morning upon the scene. By the time He had uttered the cry "Why hast thou forsaken me?," men had begun to see again, and some even ventured to misinterpret His words, more in terror than in ignorance. They said, "This man calleth for Elias" (Matt. 27:47). They may have meant a mock, but I think not. At any rate, there was no heart in what they said nor in the reply of their fellows. Yet the light had come by which they could see to dip the sponge in vinegar. Brethren, no light will ever come to dark hearts unless Jesus shall speak. And the light will not be clear until we hear the voice of His sorrows on our behalf as He cries, "Why hast thou forsaken me?" His voice of grief must be the end of our griefs. His cry out of the darkness must cheer away our gloom and bring the heavenly morning to our minds.

## The Sympathy That Prophesies

Do you see the sympathy of nature with her Lord—the sympathy of the sun in the heavens with the Sun of Righteousness? It was not possible for Him by whom all things were made to be in darkness and for nature to remain in the light.

The first sympathetic fact I see is this: *All lights are dim when Christ shines not.* All is dark when He does not shine. In the church, if Jesus is not there, what is there? The sun itself could not yield us light if Jesus were withdrawn. The seven golden lamps are ready to go out unless He walks among them and trims them with the holy oil. You soon grow heavy and your spirit faint and your hands are weary if the Christ is not with you. If Jesus Christ is not fully preached, if He is not with us by His Spirit, then everything is in darkness. Obscure the cross, and you have obscured all spiritual teaching. You cannot say, "We will clear upon every other doctrine, but we will shun the atonement, since so many cavil at it." No, sirs, if that candle is put under a bushel, the whole house is dark. All theology sympathizes with the cross and is colored and tinctured by it. Your pious service, your books, your public worship, will all be in sympathy with the cross one way or another. If the cross is in the dark, so will all your work be.

Next, *see the dependence of all creation upon Christ,* as evidenced by its darkness when He withdraws. It was not proper that He who made all worlds should die, and yet all worlds should go on just as they had done. If He suffers eclipse, they must suffer eclipse, too. If the Sun of Righteousness is made to set in blood, the natural sun must keep touch with Him. I believe that there is a much more wonderful sympathy between Christ and the world of nature than any of us have ever dreamed. The whole creation groans and travails in pain together until now, because Christ in the Church is in His travail pangs. Christ in His mystical body is in travail, and so the whole creation must wait for the manifestation of the Son of God. We are waiting for the coming of the Lord from heaven, and there is no hill or dale, there is no mountain or sea, but what is in perfect harmony with the waiting Church.

Wonder not that there should be earthquakes in divers places, blazing volcanoes, terrible tempests, and sore spreadings of deadly disease. Marvel not when you hear of dire portents, and things that make one's heart to quail, for such things must be till the end shall come. Until the great Shepherd shall make His crook into a scepter and shall begin His unsuffering reign, this poor earth must bleed at every vein. There must be darkness till these days of delay are ended. You who expect placid history till Christ shall come, expect you know not what. You who think that generous politics shall create order and content and that the extension of free trade shall breathe universal peace over the nations, look for the living among the dead. Till the Lord shall come, the word has gone out, "Overturn, overturn, overturn" (Ezek. 21:27). And overturned all things must be. Not only in other kingdoms but in this also, till Jesus comes. All that can be shaken shall be shaken, and only His immovable throne and truth shall abide. Now is the time of the Lord's battle with darkness, and we may not hope as yet for unbroken light.

Dear friend, the sin that darkened Christ and made Him die in the dark darkens the whole world. The sin that darkened Christ and made Him hang upon the cross in the dark is darkening you who do not believe in Him, and you will live in the dark and die in the dark unless you get to Him who only is the light of the world and can give light to you. There is no light for any man except in Christ. And till you believe in Him, thick darkness shall blind you, and you shall stumble in it and perish. That is the lesson I would have you learn.

Another practical lesson is this: If we are in the dark at this time, if our spirits are sunk in gloom, let us not despair, for the Lord Christ Himself was there. If I have fallen into misery on account of sin, let me not give up all hope, for the Father's Well-beloved passed through denser darkness than mine. O believing soul, if you are in the dark, you are near the King's cellars, and there are wines on the lees well refined lying there. You have gotten into the pavilion of the Lord, and now you may speak with Him. You will not find Christ in the gaudy tents of pride or in the foul haunts of wickedness. You will not find Him where the dance and the flowing bowl inflame the lusts of men, but in the house of mourning you will meet the Man of Sorrows. He is not where Herodias dances or where Bernice displays her charms, but He is where the woman of a sorrowful spirit moves her lips in prayer. He is never absent where penitence sits in darkness and bewails her faults.

If you are under a cloud, feel after your Lord, if perhaps you may find Him. Stand still in your black sorrow and say, "O Lord, the preacher tells me that Your cross once stood in such darkness as this. O Jesus hear me!" He will respond to you. The Lord will look out of the pillar of the cloud and shed a light upon you. "I know their sorrows," He says. He is no stranger to heartbreak. Christ also once suffered for sin. Trust Him, and He will cause His light to shine upon you. Lean upon Him, and He will bring you up out of the gloomy wilderness into the land of rest. God help you to do so!

*I have chosen this subject that it may help the children of God to understand a little of their infinite obligations to their redeeming Lord. You shall measure the height of His love, if it is ever measured, by the depth of His grief, if that can ever be known. See with what a price He has redeemed us from the curse of the law! As you see this, say to yourself: What manner of people should we be? What measure of love should we return to One who bore the utmost penalty, that we might be delivered from the wrath to come? I do not profess that I can dive into this deep. I will only venture to the edge of the precipice, and bid you look down, and pray the Spirit of God to concentrate your mind upon this lamentation of our dying Lord as it rises up through the thick darkness. "My God, my God, why hast thou forsaken me?"*

# Chapter Seven

# "Lama Sabachthani?"

*And about the ninth hour Jesus cried with a loud voice, saying, Eli, Eli, lama sabachthani? that is to say, My God, my God, why hast thou forsaken me?*—Matthew 27:46.

"THERE WAS DARKNESS OVER all the land unto the ninth hour" (Matt. 27:45). This cry of Jesus from the cross came out of that darkness. Expect not to see through its every word, as though it came from on high as a beam from the unclouded Sun of Righteousness. There is light in it, bright, flashing light. But there is a center of impenetrable gloom, where the soul is ready to faint because of the terrible darkness.

Our Lord was then in the darkest part of His way. He had trodden the winepress now for hours, and the work was almost finished. He had reached the culminating point of His anguish. This is His dolorous lament from the lowest pit of misery—"My God, my God, why hast thou forsaken me?" I do not think that the records of time, or even of eternity, contain a sentence more full of anguish. Here the wormwood and the gall, and all the other bitterness, are outdone. Here you may look as into a vast abyss, and though you strain your eyes and gaze till sight fails you, yet you perceive no bottom. It is measureless, unfathomable, inconceivable. This anguish of the Savior on your behalf and mine is no more to be measured and weighed than the sin that required it or the love that endured it. We will adore where we cannot comprehend.

I have chosen this subject that it may help the children of God to understand a little of their infinite obligations to their redeeming Lord. You shall measure the height of His love, if it is ever measured, by the depth of His grief, if that can ever be known. See with what a price He has redeemed us from the curse of the law! As you see this, say to yourself: What manner of people should we be? What measure of love should we return to One who bore the utmost penalty, that we might be delivered from the wrath to come? I do not profess that I can dive into this deep. I will only venture to the edge of the precipice, and bid you look down, and pray the Spirit of God to concentrate your mind upon this lamentation of our dying Lord as it rises up through the thick darkness. "My God, my God, why hast thou forsaken me?"

Our first subject of thought will be *the fact* of what He suffered—God had forsaken Him. Second, we will note *the inquiry* about why He suffered. This word *why* is the edge of the text. "Why hast thou forsaken me?" Then, third, we will consider *the answer* of what came of His suffering. The answer flowed softly into the soul of the Lord Jesus without the need of words, for He ceased from His anguish with the triumphant shout of, "It is finished." His work was finished, and His bearing of desertion was a chief part of the work He had undertaken for our sake.

## The Fact

By the help of the Holy Spirit, let us first dwell upon *the fact* of what our Lord suffered. God had forsaken Him. Grief of mind is harder to bear than pain of body. You can pluck up courage and endure the pang of sickness and pain, so long as the spirit is strong and brave. But if the soul itself is touched, and the mind becomes diseased with anguish, then every pain is increased in severity, and there is nothing with which to sustain it. Spiritual sorrows are the worst of mental miseries. A man may bear great depression of spirit about worldly matters if he feels that he has his God to go to. He is cast down but not in despair. Like David, he dialogues with himself, and he enquires, "Why art thou cast down, O my soul? and why art thou disquieted in me? hope thou in God: for I shall yet praise him!" (Ps. 42:5). But if the Lord is once withdrawn, if the comfortable light of His presence is shadowed even for an hour, there is a torment within the breast that I can only liken to the prelude of hell. This is the greatest of all weights that can press upon the heart. This made the psalmist plead, "Hide not thy face far from me; put not thy servant away in anger" (Ps. 27:9). We can bear a bleeding body and even a wounded spirit, but a soul conscious of desertion by God is beyond conception unendurable. When He holds back the face of His throne and spreads His cloud upon it, who can endure the darkness?

This voice out of "the belly of hell" marks the lowest depth of the Savior's grief. *The desertion was real.* Though under some aspects our Lord could say, "The Father is with me," yet was it solemnly true that God did forsake Him. It was not a failure of faith on His part that led Him to imagine what was not actual fact. Our faith fails us, and then we think that God has forsaken us; but our Lord's faith did not for a moment falter, for He says twice, "*My* God, *my* God." Oh, the mighty double grip of His unhesitating faith! He seems to say, "Even if You have forsaken me, I have not forsaken You." Faith triumphs, and there is no sign of any faintness of heart toward the living God. Yet, strong as is His faith, He feels that God has withdrawn His comfortable fellowship, and He shivers under the terrible deprivation.

It was no deception or delirium of mind caused by His weakness of body, the heat of the fever, the depression of His spirit, or the near approach of death. He was clear of mind even to this last. He bore up under pain, loss of blood, scorn, thirst, and desolation, making no complaint of the cross, the nails, and the scoffing. We read not in the gospels of anything more than the natural cry of weakness: "I thirst." All the tortures of His body He endured in silence. But when it came to being forsaken of God, then His great heart burst out into its "Lama sabachthani?" His one moan is concerning His God. Is it not, "Why has Peter denied me? Why has Judas betrayed me?" These were sharp griefs, but this is the sharpest. This stroke has cut Him to the quick: "My God, my God, why hast *thou* forsaken me?" It was no phantom of the gloom, but it was a real absence that He mourned.

This was *a very remarkable desertion.* It is not the way of God to leave either His sons or His servants. His saints, when they come to die, in their great weakness and pain, find Him near. They are made to sing because of the presence of God: "Yea, though I walk through the valley of the shadow of death, I will fear no evil: for thou art with me" (Ps. 23:4). Dying saints have clear visions of the living God. Our observation has taught us that if the Lord is away at other times, He is never absent from His people at the time of death or in the furnace of affliction. Concerning the three holy children, we do not read that the Lord was ever visibly with them till they walked the fires of Nebuchadnezzar's furnace; but there and then the Lord met with them (Dan. 3:25). Yes, beloved, it is God's desire to keep company with His afflicted people, and yet He forsook His Son in the hour of His tribulation! How usual it is to see the Lord with His faithful witnesses when resisting even unto blood! Read *Foxe's Book of Martyrs,* and I care not whether you study the early or the later persecutions, you will find them all lit up with the evident presence of the Lord with His witnesses. Did the Lord ever fail to support a martyr at the stake? Did He ever forsake one of His testifiers upon the scaffold? The testimony of the Church has always been that while the Lord has permitted His saints to suffer in body, He has so divinely sustained their spirits that they have been more than conquerors and have treated their sufferings as light afflictions. The fire has not been a bed of roses, but it has been a chariot of victory. The sword is sharp, and death is bitter; but the love of Christ is sweet, and to die for Him has been turned into glory. No, it is not God's way to forsake His champions or to leave even the least of His children in the trial hour.

As to our Lord, this forsaking was *singular.* Did His Father ever leave Him before? Will you read the four evangelists through and find any previous instance in which He complains of His Father having forsaken Him? No. He said, "I knew that thou hearest me always" (John 11:42). He lived in constant touch with God. His fellowship with the Father was always near and dear and clear. But now, for the first time, He cries, "Why hast thou forsaken me?" It was very remarkable. It was a riddle only to be solved by the fact that He loved us and gave Himself for us and, in the execution of His loving purpose, came even unto this sorrow of mourning the absence of His God.

This forsaking was *very terrible.* Who can fully tell what it is to be forsaken of God? We can only form a guess by what we have ourselves felt under temporary and partial desertion. God has never left us completely, for He has expressly said, "I will never leave thee, nor forsake thee" (Heb. 13:5). Yet we have sometimes felt as if He had cast us off. We have cried, "Oh that I knew where I might find him!" (Job 23:3). The clear shinings of His love have been withdrawn. Thus we are able to form some little idea of how the Savior felt when His God had forsaken Him. The mind of Jesus was left to dwell upon one dark subject, and no cheering theme consoled Him. It was the hour in which He was made to stand before God as consciously the sin bearer, according to that ancient prophecy: "The Lord hath laid on him the iniquity of us all" (Isa. 53:6). Then was it true: "He hath made him to be sin for us" (2 Cor. 5:21). Peter puts it: "[He] his own self bare our sins in his own body on the tree" (1 Pet. 2:24). Sin, sin, sin was everywhere around and about Christ. He had no sin of His own. He had no strength given Him from on high, no secret oil and wine poured into His wounds. But He was made to appear in the lone character of the Lamb of God which taketh away the sin of the world. Therefore, He must feel the weight of sin and the turning away of that sacred face that cannot look thereon.

His Father at that time gave Him no open acknowledgement. On certain other occasions, a voice had been heard, saying, "This is my beloved Son, in whom I am well pleased" (Matt. 17:5). But now, when such a testimony seemed most of all required, the oracle was silent. He was hung up as an accursed thing upon the cross, for He was "made a curse for us: for it is written, Cursed is every one that hangeth on a tree" (Gal. 3:13). Yet the Lord His God did not own Him before men. If it had pleased the Father, He might have sent Him twelve legions of angels, but not an angel came after the Christ had left Gethsemane. His despisers might spit in His face, but no swift seraph came to avenge the indignity. They might bind Him and scourge Him, but none of all the heavenly host would interpose to screen His shoulders from the lash. They might fasten Him to the tree with nails and lift Him up and scoff at Him, but no cohort of ministering spirits hastened to drive back the rabble and release the Prince of life. No, He appeared to be forsaken, "smitten of God, and afflicted" (Isa. 53:4), delivered into the hands of cruel men, whose wicked hands worked Him misery without stint. Well might He ask, "My God, my God, why hast thou forsaken me?"

But this was not all. His Father now dried up that sacred stream of peaceful communion and loving fellowship that had flowed throughout His whole earthly life. He said Himself, as you remember, "Ye shall be scattered, every man to his own, and shall leave me alone: and yet I am not alone, because the Father is with me" (John 16:32). Here was His constant comfort, but all comfort from this source was to be withdrawn. The divine Spirit did not minister to His human spirit. No communications with His Father's love poured into His heart. It was not possible that the Judge should smile upon the One who represented the prisoner at the bar of justice. Our Lord's faith did not fail Him, as I have already shown you, for He said, "My God, my God"; yet no sensible supports were given to His heart, and no comforts were poured into His mind. One writer declares that Jesus did not taste of divine wrath but only suffered a withdrawal of divine fellowship. What is the difference? Whether God withdraws heat or creates cold, it is the same. He was neither smiled upon nor allowed to feel that He was near to God. And this, to His tender spirit, was grief of the keenest order. Our Lord suffered to the extreme point of deprivation. He had not the light that makes existence to be life, and life to be a blessing. You who know, in your degree, what it is to lose the conscious presence and love of God, you can faintly guess what the sorrow of the Savior was, now that He felt He had been forsaken of His God. "If the foundations be destroyed, what can the righteous do?" (Ps. 11:3). To our Lord, the Father's love was the foundation of everything. When that was gone, all was gone. Nothing remained within, without, above, when His own God, the God of His entire confidence, turned from Him. Yes, God in very deed forsook our Savior.

To be forsaken of God was *much more a source of anguish to Jesus than it would be to us.* "Oh," say you, "how is that?" I answer, because He was perfectly holy. A rupture between a perfectly holy being and the thrice holy God must be in the highest degree strange, abnormal, perplexing, and painful. If any man who is not at peace with God could only know his true condition, he would swoon with fright. If you unforgiven ones only knew where you are and what you are at this moment in the sight of God, you would never smile again till you were reconciled to Him. Alas, we are insensible, hardened by the deceitfulness of sin, and therefore we do not feel our true condition! His perfect holiness made it to our Lord a dreadful calamity to be forsaken of the thrice holy God.

I remember, also, that our blessed Lord had lived in unbroken fellowship with God, and to be forsaken was a new grief to Him. He had never known what the dark was till then. His life had been lived in the light of God. Think, dear child of God, if you had always dwelt in full communion with God, your days would have been as the days of heaven upon earth; and how cold it would strike to your heart to find yourself in the darkness of desertion. If you can conceive such a thing as happening to a perfect man, you can see why to our Well-Beloved it was a special trial. Remember, He had enjoyed fellowship with God more richly as well as more constantly than any of us. His fellowship with the Father was of the highest, deepest, fullest order; and what must the loss of it have been? We lose but drops when we lose our joyful experience of heavenly fellowship, and yet the loss is killing. But to our Lord Jesus Christ, the sea was dried up—I mean His sea of fellowship with the infinite God.

Do not forget that He was such a One that to Him to be without God must have been an overwhelming calamity. In every part He was perfect, and in every part fitted for communion with God to a supreme degree. A sinful man has an awful need of God, but he does not know it. Therefore, he does not feel that hunger and thirst after God that would come upon a perfect man could he be deprived of God. The very perfection of His nature renders it inevitable that the holy man must either be in communion with God or be desolate. Imagine a stray angel, a seraph who has lost his God! Conceive him to be perfect in holiness and yet to have fallen into a condition in which he cannot find his God! I cannot picture him. Perhaps a Milton might have done so. He is sinless and trustful, and yet he has an overpowering feeling that God is absent from him. He has drifted into the nowhere—the unimaginable region behind the back of God. I think I hear the wailing of the cherub: "My God, my God, my God, where are You?" What a sorrow for one of the sons of the morning! But here we have the lament of a being far more capable of fellowship with the Godhead. In proportion as He is more fitted to receive the love of the great Father, in that proportion is His pining after it the more intense. As a Son, He is more able to commune with God than ever a servant angel could be. And now that He is forsaken of God, the void within is the greater and the anguish more bitter.

Our Lord's heart and all His nature were, morally and spiritually, so delicately formed, so sensitive, so tender that to be without God was to Him a grief that could not be weighed. I see Him in the text bearing desertion, and yet I perceive that He cannot bear it. I know not how to express my meaning except by such a paradox. He cannot endure to be without God. He had surrendered Himself to be left of God, as the representative of sinners must be, but His pure and holy nature, after three hours of silence, finds the position unendurable to love and purity. Breaking forth from it, now that the hour was over, He exclaims, "Why hast thou forsaken me?" He quarrels not with the suffering, but He cannot abide in the position that caused it. He seems as if He must end the ordeal, not because of the pain but because of the moral shock. We have here the repetition after His passion of that loathing that He felt before it, when He cried, "If it be possible, let this cup pass from me: nevertheless not as I will, but as thou wilt" (Matt. 26:39). "My God, my God, why hast thou forsaken me?" is the holiness of Christ amazed at the position of substitute for guilty men.

## The Inquiry

Note carefully this cry: "My God, my God, why hast thou forsaken me?" It is pure anguish, undiluted agony, that cries like this. But it is the agony of a godly soul, for only a man of that order would have used such an expression. Let us learn from it useful lessons. This cry is taken from "the Book." Does it not show our Lord's love of the sacred volume, that when He felt His sharpest grief, He turned to the Scripture to find a fit utterance for it? Here we have the opening sentence of the twenty-second psalm. Oh, that we may so love the inspired Word that we may not only sing to its score but even weep to its music!

Note, again, that our Lord's lament is an address to God. The godly, in their anguish, turn to the hand that smites them. The Savior's outcry is not *against* God but *to* God. "My God, my God." He makes a double effort to draw near. True Sonship is here. The child in the dark is crying after His Father, "My God, my God." Both the Bible and prayer were dear to Jesus in His agony.

Still, observe, it is a faith cry, for though it asks, "Why hast thou forsaken me?" yet it first says, twice over, "My God, my God." The grip of appropriation is in the word *my*, but the reverence of humility is in the word *God*. It is " 'My *God*, my *God*,' You are my *God*. You can do as you will, and I yield to Your sacred sovereignty. I kiss the hand that smites me, and with all my heart I cry, 'My God, my God.'" When you are delirious with pain, think of your Bible still. When your mind wanders, let it roam toward the mercy seat. And when your heart and your flesh fail, still live by faith, and still cry, "My God, my God."

Let us come close to the inquiry. It looked to me, at first sight, like *a question of one distraught*, driven from the balance of His mind—not unreasonable, but too much reasoning, and therefore tossed about. "Why hast thou forsaken me?" Did not Jesus know? Did He not know why He was forsaken? He knew it most distinctly, and yet His manhood, while it was being crushed, pounded, dissolved, seemed as though it could not understand the reason for so great a grief. He must be forsaken, but could there be a sufficient cause for so sickening a sorrow? The cup must be bitter, but why this most nauseous of ingredients? I tremble lest I say what I should not say. I have said it, and I think there is truth—the Man of Sorrows was overborne with horror. At that moment, the finite soul of the man Christ Jesus came into awful contact with the infinite justice of God. The one Mediator between God and man, the man Christ Jesus, beheld the holiness of God in arms against the sin of man, whose nature He had espoused. God was for Him and with Him in a certain unquestionable sense; but for the time, so far as His feeling went, God was against Him and necessarily withdrawn from Him. It is not surprising that the holy soul of Christ should shudder at finding itself brought into painful contact with the infinite justice of God, even though its design was only to vindicate that justice and glorify the Law Giver. Our Lord could now say, "All thy waves and thy billows are gone over me" (Ps. 42:7). Therefore, He uses language that is all too hot with anguish to be dissected by the cold hand of a logical criticism. Grief has small regard for the laws of the grammarian. Even the holiest, when in extreme agony, though they cannot speak otherwise than according to purity and truth, use a language of their own that only the ear of sympathy can fully receive. I see not all that is here, but what I can see I am not able to put into words for you.

I think I see, in the expression, *submission and resolve.* Our Lord does not draw back. There is a forward movement in the question. Those who quit a business ask no more questions about it. He does not ask that the forsaking may end prematurely. He would only understand anew its meaning. He does not shrink, but He rather dedicates Himself anew to God by the words, "My God, my God," and by seeking to review the ground and reason of that anguish that He is resolute to bear even to the bitter end. He yearns to feel fresh the motive that has sustained Him and must sustain Him to the end. The cry sounds to me like deep submission and strong resolve, pleasing with God.

Do you not think that *the amazement of our Lord,* when He was made to be sin for us (2 Cor. 5:21), led Him thus to cry out? For such a sacred and pure being to be made a sin offering was an amazing experience. Sin was laid on Him, and He was treated as if He had been guilty, though He had personally never sinned. Now the infinite horror of rebellion against the most holy God fills His holy soul, the unrighteousness of sin breaks His heart, and He starts back from it, crying, "My God, my God, why hast thou forsaken me?" Why must I bear the dread result of conduct I so much abhor?

Do you not see, moreover, there was here *a glance at His eternal purpose and at His secret source of joy?* That *why* is the silver lining of the dark cloud, and our Lord looked wishfully at it. He knew that the desertion was needful so that He might save the guilty, and He had an eye to that salvation as His comfort. He is not forsaken needlessly nor without a worthy design. The design is in itself so dear to His heart that He yields to the passing evil even though that evil is like death to Him. He looks at that *why*, and through that narrow window, the light of heaven comes streaming into His darkened life.

"My God, my God, why hast thou forsaken me?" Surely our Lord dwelt on that *why, that we might also turn our eyes that way.* He would have us see the why and the wherefore of His grief. He would have us mark the gracious motive for its endurance. Think much of all your Lord suffered, but do not overlook the reason for it. If you cannot always understand how this or that grief worked toward the great end of the whole passion, yet believe that it has a share in the grand *why.* Make a life study of that bitter but blessed question: "Why hast thou forsaken me?" Thus, the Savior raises an inquiry not so much for Himself as for us, and not so much because of a hope and a joy set before Him, which were wells of comfort to Him in His wilderness of woe.

Do you think for a moment that the Lord God, in the broadest and most unreserved sense, could never, in very deed, have forsaken His most obedient Son? He was ever with Him in the grand design of salvation. Toward the Lord Jesus, personally, God Himself, personally, must ever have stood on terms of infinite love. Truly the Only Begotten was never more lovely to the Father than when He was obedient unto death, even the death of the cross! But we must look upon God here as the Judge of all the earth, and we must look upon the Lord Jesus also in His official capacity, as the Surety of the covenant and the Sacrifice for sin. The great Judge of all cannot smile upon Him who has become the Substitute for the guilty. Sin is loathed of God; and if, for its removal, His own Son is made to bear it, yet, as sin, it is still loathsome, and He who bears it cannot be in happy communion with God. This was the dread necessity of expiation. But in the essence of things, the love of the great Father to His Son never ceased or ever knew a diminution. Restrained in its flow it must be, but lessened at its fountainhead it could not be. Therefore, wonder not at the question "Why hast thou forsaken me?"

## The Answer

What is the outcome of this suffering? What was the reason for it? Our Savior could answer His own question. If for a moment His manhood was perplexed, yet His mind soon came to clear apprehension, for He said, "It is finished." And as I have already said, He then referred to the work that in His lonely agony He had been performing. Why, then, did God forsake His Son? I cannot conceive any other answer than this: *He stood in our place.* There was no reason in Christ why the Father should forsake Him: He was perfect, and His life was without spot. God never acts without reason; and since there were no reasons in the character and person of the Lord Jesus why His Father should forsake Him, we must look elsewhere. I do not know how others answer the question. I can only answer it in this one way:

> *Yet all the griefs He felt were ours,*
> *Ours were the woes He bore;*
> *Pangs, not His own, His spotless soul*
> *With bitter anguish tore.*

> *We held Him as condemn'd of heaven,*
> *An outcast from His God;*
> *While for our sins, He groaned, He bled,*
> *Beneath His Father's rod.*

He bore the sinner's sin, and He therefore had to be treated as though He were a sinner, though sinner He could never be. With His own full consent He suffered as though He had committed the transgressions that were laid on Him. Our sin, and His taking it upon Himself, is the answer to the question "Why hast thou forsaken me?"

In this case we now see that *His obedience was perfect*. He came into the world to obey the Father, and He rendered that obedience to the very uttermost. The spirit of obedience could go no further than for one who feels forsaken of God still to cling to Him in solemn, avowed allegiance, still declaring before a mocking multitude His confidence in the afflicting God. It is noble to cry, "my God, my God," when one is asking, "Why hast thou forsaken me?" How much further can obedience go? I see nothing beyond it. The soldier at the gate of Pompeii, remaining at his post as sentry when the shower of burning ashes is falling, is not more true to his trust than He who adheres to a forsaking God with loyalty of hope.

*Our Lord's suffering in this particular form was appropriate and necessary.* It would not have sufficed for our Lord merely to have been pained in body or even to have been grieved in mind in other ways. He must suffer in this particular way. He must feel forsaken of God because this is the necessary consequence of sin. For a man to be forsaken of God is the penalty that naturally and inevitably follows upon his breaking his relation with God. What is death? What was the death that was threatened to Adam? "In the day that thou eatest thereof thou shalt surely die" (Gen. 2:17). Is death annihilation? Was Adam annihilated that day? Assuredly not, for he lived many years afterward. But in the day in which he ate of the forbidden fruit he died by being separated from God. The separation of the soul from God is spiritual death, just as the separation of the soul from the body is natural death. The sacrifice for sin must be put in the place of separation and must bow to the penalty of death. By this placing of the great Sacrifice under forsaking and death, it would be seen by all creatures throughout the universe that God could not have fellowship with sin. If even the Holy One, who stood the Just for the unjust, found God forsaking Him, what must the doom of the actual sinner be! Sin is evidently always, in every case, a dividing influence, putting even the Christ Himself, as a sin bearer, in the place of distance.

This was necessary for another reason. There could have been no laying on of suffering for sin without the forsaking of the vicarious Sacrifice by the Lord God. So long as the smile of God rests on the man, the law is not afflicting him. The approving look of the great Judge cannot fall upon a man who is viewed as standing in the place of the guilty. Christ suffered not only *from* sin but also *for* sin. If God will cheer and sustain Him, He is not suffering for sin.

The Judge is not inflicting suffering for sin if He is manifestly suc-
coring the smitten one. There could have been no vicarious suffering on the part of Christ for human guilt if He had continued
consciously to enjoy the full sunshine of the Father's presence. It
was essential to being a victim in our place that He should cry,
"My God, my God, why has thou forsaken me?"

Beloved, see how marvelously, in the person of Christ, the Lord
our God has vindicated His law! If to make His law glorious, He
had said, "These multitudes of men have broken My law, and
therefore they shall perish," the law would have been terribly magnified. But, instead thereof, He says, "Here is My Only Begotten
Son, My other self. He takes on Himself the nature of these rebellious creatures, and He consents that I should lay on Him the load
of their iniquity and visit in His person the offenses that might have
been punished in the persons of all these multitudes of men. And I
will have it so." When Jesus bows His head to the stroke of the law,
when He submissively consents that His Father shall turn away
His face from Him, the myriads of worlds are astonished at the perfect holiness and stern justice of the Lawgiver. There are, probably,
worlds innumerable throughout the boundless creation of God,
and all these will see, in the death of God's dear Son, a declaration
of His determination never to allow sin to be trifled with. If His
own Son is brought before Him, bearing the sin of others upon
Him, He will hide His face from Him as well as from the actually
guilty. In God infinite love shines over all, but it does not eclipse
His absolute justice any more than His justice is permitted to
destroy His love. God has all perfections in perfection, and in
Christ Jesus we see the reflection of them. Beloved, this is a wonderful theme! Oh, that I had a pen worthy of this subject, but who
could ever reach the height of this great argument?

Once more, when inquiring, Why did Jesus suffer to be forsaken of the Father?, we see the fact that *the Captain of our salvation
was thus made perfect through suffering.* Every part of the road has
been traversed by our Lord's own feet. Suppose, beloved, the Lord
Jesus had never been thus forsaken. Then one of His disciples
might have been called to that sharp endurance, and the Lord Jesus
could not have sympathized with him in it. The disciple would
turn to his Leader and Captain and say to Him, "Did You, my Lord,
ever feel this darkness?" Then the Lord Jesus would answer, "No.
This is a descent such as I never made." What a dreadful lack

would the tried one have felt! For the servant to bear a grief his Master never knew would be sad indeed. There would have been a wound for which there was no ointment, a pint for which there was no balm. But it is not so now. "In all their affliction he was afflicted" (Isa. 63:9). "[He] was in all points tempted like as we are, yet without sin" (Heb. 4:15). Wherein we greatly rejoice at this time, and so often as we are cast down, underneath us is the deep experience of our forsaken Lord.

I will finish when I have said three things. The first is, you and I who are believers in the Lord Jesus Christ and are resting in Him alone for salvation, *let us lean hard,* let us bear with all our weight on our Lord. He will bear the full weight of all our sin and care. As to my sin, I hear its harsh accusings no more when I hear Jesus cry, "Why hast thou forsaken me?" I know that I deserve the deepest hell at the hand of God's justice, but I am not afraid. He will never forsake *me,* for He forsook His Son on my behalf. I shall not suffer for my sin, for Jesus has suffered to the full in my place. Behind this brazen wall of substitution a sinner is safe. These munitions of rock guard all believers, who may rest secure. The rock is cleft of me. I hide in its rifts, and no harm can reach me. You have a full atonement, a great sacrifice, a glorious vindication of the law. Therefore, rest at peace, all you who put your trust in Jesus.

Next, if ever in our lives henceforth we should think that God has deserted us, *let us learn from our Lord's example how to behave ourselves.* If God has left you, do not shut up your Bible. Nay, open it, as your Lord did and find a text that will suit you. If God has left you, or you think so, do not give up prayer. Nay, pray as your Lord did, and be more earnest than ever. If you think God has forsaken you, do not give up your faith in Him, but like your Lord, cry, "My God, my God," again and again. If you have had one anchor before, cast out two anchors now and double the hold of your faith. If you cannot call Jehovah "Father," as Christ did, call Him your "God." Let the pronouns take their hold: "My God, my God." Let nothing drive you from your faith. Still hold on to Jesus, sink or swim. As for me, if ever I am lost, it shall be at the foot of the cross. To this pass have I come that if I never see the face of God with acceptance, yet I will believe that He will be faithful to His Son and true to the covenant sealed by oaths and blood. He who believes in Jesus has everlasting life: There I cling, like the limpet to the rock. There is but one gate of heaven, and even if I may not enter it, I will cling to the posts of its door. What am I saying? I shall enter in, for that gate was never shut against a soul that accepted Jesus. And Jesus saith, "Him that cometh to me I will in no wise cast out" (John 6:37).

The last of the three points is this: *Let us abhor the sin that brought such agony upon our beloved Lord.* What an accursed thing is sin that crucified the Lord Jesus! Do you laugh at it? Will you go and spend an evening to see a mimic performance of it? Do you roll sin under your tongue as a sweet morsel and then come to God's house on Sunday morning and think to worship Him? Worship Him! Worship Him, with sin indulged in your breast! Worship Him, with sin loved and pampered in your life! If I had a dear brother who had been murdered, what would you think of me if I valued the knife that had been crimsoned with his blood? If I made a friend of the murderer and daily consorted with the assassin who drove the dagger into my brother's heart, what would you think of me? Surely I, too, must be an accomplice in the crime!

Sin murdered Christ; will you be a friend to it? Sin pierced the heart of the Incarnate God; can you love it? Oh, that there was an abyss as deep as Christ's misery, that I might at once hurl this dagger of sin into its depths, whence it might never be brought to light again! Begone, O sin! You are banished from the heart where Jesus reigns! Begone, for you have crucified my Lord and made Him cry, "Why hast thou forsaken me?" If you did but know yourself and know the love of Christ, you would vow that you would harbor sin no longer. You would be indignant at sin, and cry:

> *The dearest idol I have known,*
> *Whate'er that idol be,*
> *Lord, I will tear it from its throne,*
> *And worship only Thee.*

May the Christ who suffered for you bless you, and out of His darkness may your light arise! Amen.

$W$hile we admire His condescension, let our thoughts also turn with delight to His sure sympathy. If Jesus said, "I thirst," then He knows all our frailties and woes. The next time we are in pain or are suffering depression of spirit, we will remember that our Lord understands it all, for He has had practical, personal experience of it. Neither in torture of body nor in sadness of heart are we deserted by our Lord. His line is parallel with ours. The arrow that has lately pierced you was first stained with His blood. The cup that you are made to drink, though it is very bitter, bears the mark of His lips about its brim. He has traversed the mournful way before you, and every footprint you leave in the sodden soil is stamped side by side with His footmarks. Let the sympathy of Christ, then, be fully believed in and deeply appreciated, since He said, "I thirst."

# Chapter Eight

# The Shortest
# of the Seven Cries

*After this, Jesus knowing that all things were now accomplished,*
*that the scripture might be fulfilled, saith, I thirst—John 19:28.*

IT WAS MOST FITTING THAT every word
of our Lord upon the cross should be gathered up and preserved.
As not a bone of Him shall be broken, so not a word shall be lost.
The Holy Spirit took special care that each of the sacred utterances
should be fittingly recorded. There were seven of those last words,
and seven is the number of perfection and fullness. It is the number that blends the three of the infinite God with the four of complete creation. Our Lord in His death cries, as in all else, was perfection itself. There is a fullness of meaning in each utterance that
no man shall be able fully to bring forth, and when combined they
make up a vast deep of thought, which no human line can fathom.
Here, as everywhere else, we are constrained to say of our Lord,
"Never man spake like this man" (John 7:46). Amid all the anguish
of His spirit, His last words prove Him to have remained fully self-
possessed, true to His forgiving nature, true to His kingly office,
true to His filial relationship, true to His God, true to His love of the
written word, true to His glorious work, and true to His faith in His
Father.

As these seven sayings were so faithfully recorded, we do not wonder that they have frequently been the subject of devout meditation. Fathers and confessors, preachers and divines, have delighted to dwell upon every syllable of these matchless cries. These solemn sentences have shone like the seven golden candlesticks or the seven stars of the Apocalypse and have lighted multitudes of men to Him who spoke them. Thoughtful men have drawn a wealth of meaning from them, and in so doing have arranged them into different groups and placed them under several heads. I cannot give you more than a mere taste of this rich subject, but I have been most struck with two ways of regarding our Lord's last words. First, they teach and confirm many of the doctrines of our holy faith. *"Father, forgive them; for they know not what they do"* is the first. Here is the forgiveness of sin—free forgiveness in answer to the Savior's plea. *"To day shalt thou be with me in paradise."* Here is the safety of the believer in the hour of his departure, and his instant admission into the presence of his Lord. It is a blow at the fable of purgatory that strikes it to the heart. *Woman, behold thy son!"* This very plainly sets forth the true and proper humanity of Christ, who to the end recognized His human relationship to Mary, of whom He was born. Yet His language teaches us not to worship *her*, for He calls her "woman," but to honor Him who in His direst agony thought of her needs and griefs as He also thinks of all His people, for these are His mother and sister and brother. *"Eloi, Eloi, lama sabachthani?"* is the fourth cry, and it illustrates the penalty endured by our Substitute when He bore our sins and so was forsaken of His God. The sharpness of that sentence no exposition can fully disclose to us. It is keen as the very edge and point of the sword that pierced His heart. *"I thirst"* is the fifth cry, and its utterance teaches us the truth of Scripture, for all things were accomplished that the Scripture might be fulfilled, and therefore our Lord said, "I thirst." Holy Scripture remains the basis of our faith established by every word and act of our Redeemer. The last word but one is *"It is finished."* There is the complete justification of the believer, since the work by which he is accepted is fully accomplished. The last of His last words is also taken from the Scriptures and shows where His mind was feeding. He cried before He bowed the head that He had held erect amid all His conflict, as one who never yielded, *"Father, into thy hands I commend my spirit."* In that cry there is reconciliation to God. He who stood in our stead has finished all His work, and now His spirit comes back to the Father, and He brings us with Him. Every word, therefore, you see, teaches us some grand fundamental doctrine of our blessed faith. "He that hath an ear, let him hear" (Rev. 2:7).

A second mode of treating these seven cries is to view them as setting forth the person and offices of our Lord who uttered them. *"Father, forgive them; for they know not what they do."* Here we see the Mediator interceding. Jesus stands before the Father pleading for the guilty. *"Verily I say unto thee, To day shalt thou be with me in paradise."* This is the Lord Jesus in kingly power, and opening with the key of David a door that none can shut, admitting into the gates of heaven the poor soul who had confessed Him on the tree. Hail, everlasting King in heaven, You do admit to Your paradise whomsoever You will! Nor do You set a time for waiting, but instantly You set wide the gate of pearl. You have all power in heaven as well as upon earth. Then came, *"Woman, behold thy son!"* wherein we see the Son of man in the gentleness of a son caring for His bereaved mother. In the former cry, as He opened paradise, you saw the Son of God; now you see Him who was verily and truly born of a woman, made under the law. And under the law you see Him still, for He honors His mother and cares for her in the last article of death. Then comes the *"My God, my God why hast thou forsaken me?"* Here we behold His human soul in anguish, His inmost heart overwhelmed by the withdrawing of Jehovah's face and made to cry out as if in perplexity and amazement. *"I thirst"* is His human *body* tormented by grievous pain. Here you see how the mortal flesh had to share in the agony of the inward spirit. *"It is finished"* is the last word but one, and there you see the perfected Savior, the Captain of our salvation, who has completed the undertaking upon which He had entered, finished transgression, made an end of sin, and brought in everlasting righteousness. The last expiring word, in which He *commended His spirit to His Father*, is the note of acceptance for Himself and for us all. As He commends His spirit into the Father's hand, so does He bring all believers nigh unto God, and henceforth we are in the hand of the Father, who is greater than all, and none shall pluck us away. Is not this a fertile field of thought? May the Holy Spirit often lead us to glean therein.

There are many other ways in which these words might be read, and they would be found to be all full of instruction. Like the steps of a ladder or the links of a golden chain, there is a mutual dependence and interlinking of each of the cries, so that one leads to another and that to a third. Separately or in connection, our Master's words overflow with instruction to thoughtful minds.

Our text is the shortest of all the words of Calvary. It stands as two words in our language, "I thirst," but in the Greek it is only one. I cannot say that it is short and sweet, for alas, it was bitterness itself to our Lord Jesus. And yet out of its bitterness I trust there will come great sweetness to us. Though bitter to Him in the speaking, it will be sweet to us in the hearing—so sweet that all the bitterness of our trials shall be forgotten as we remember the vinegar and gall that He drank.

## The Ensign of His True Humanity

Jesus said, "I thirst," and this is the complaint of a man. Our Lord is the Maker of the ocean and the waters that are above the firmament. It is His hand that stays or opens the bottles of heaven and sends rain upon the evil and upon the good. "The sea is his, and he made it" (Ps. 95:5), and all fountains and springs are of His digging. He pours out the streams that run among the hills, the torrents that rush down the mountains, and the flowing rivers that enrich the plains. One would have said, "If He were thirsty He would not tell us, for all the clouds and rains would be glad to refresh His brow, and the brooks and streams would joyously flow at His feet." And yet, though He was Lord of all, He had so fully taken upon Himself the form of a servant and was so perfectly made in the likeness of sinful flesh that He cried with fainting voice, "I thirst." How truly man He is. He is indeed, "bone of our bone and flesh of our flesh," for He bears our infirmities. I invite you to meditate upon the true humanity of our Lord very reverently and very lovingly. Jesus was proved to be really man, because He suffered the pains that belong to manhood. Angels cannot suffer thirst. A phantom, as some have called Him, could not suffer in this fashion. But Jesus really suffered, not only the more refined pains of delicate and sensitive minds but also the rougher and commoner pangs of flesh and blood. Thirst is a commonplace misery, such as may happen to anyone. It is real pain and not a thing of a fancy or a nightmare of dreamland. Thirst is no royal grief but an evil of universal manhood. Jesus is brother to the poorest and most humble of our race.

Our Lord, however, endured thirst to an extreme degree, for it was the thirst of death that was upon Him, and more, it was the thirst of One whose death was not a common one, for "he by the grace of God should taste death for every man" (Heb. 2:9). That thirst was caused perhaps in part by the loss of blood and by the fever created by the irritation caused by His four grievous wounds. The nails were fastened in the most sensitive parts of the body, and the wounds were widened as the weight of His body dragged the nails through His blessed flesh and tore His tender nerves. The extreme tension produced a burning feverishness. It was pain that dried His mouth and made it like an oven, till He declared, in the language of the twenty-second psalm, "My tongue cleaveth to my jaws" (vs. 15). It was a thirst such as none of us have ever known, for not yet has the death dew condensed upon our brows. We shall perhaps know it in our measure in our dying hour, but not yet, nor ever so terribly as He did. Our Lord felt that grievous drought of dissolution by which all moisture seems dried up and the flesh returns to the dust of death. This is known by those who have commenced to tread the valley of the shadow of death. Jesus, being a man, escaped none of the ills that are allotted to man in death. He is indeed, "Emmanuel,…God with us" (Matt. 1:23), everywhere.

Believing this, let us tenderly feel how very near akin to us our Lord Jesus has become. You have been ill, and you have been parched with fever as He was, and then you too have gasped out, "I thirst." Your path runs hard by that of your Master. He said, "I thirst," so that someone might bring Him drink, even as you have wished to have a cooling draught handed to you when you could not help yourself. Can you help feeling how very near Jesus is to us when His lips must be moistened with a sponge and He must be so dependent upon others as to ask for drink from their hand? Next time your fevered lips murmur, "I am very thirsty," you may say to yourself, "Those are sacred words, for my Lord spoke in that fashion." The words, "I thirst," are a common voice in death chambers. We can never forget the painful scenes of which we have been witness when we have watched the dissolving of the human frame. Some of those whom we loved very dearly have been unable to help themselves. The death sweat has been upon them, and this has been one of the marks of their approaching death, that they have been parched with thirst and could only mutter between their half-closed lips, "Give me a drink." Ah, beloved, our Lord was so truly man that all our griefs remind us of Him. The next time we are thirsty, we may gaze upon Him. And whenever we see a friend faint and thirsting while dying, we may behold our Lord dimly but truly mirrored in His members. How near akin the thirsty Savior is to us. Let us love Him more and more.

How great the love that led Him to such a condescension as this! Do not let us forget the infinite distance between the Lord of glory on His throne and the Crucified dried up with thirst. A river of the water of life, pure as crystal, proceeds today out of the throne of God and of the Lamb, and yet once He condescended to say, "I thirst." He is Lord of fountains and all deeps, but not a cup of cold water was placed to His lips. Oh, if He had at any time said, "I thirst," before His angelic guards, they would surely have emulated the courage of the men of David when they cut their way to the well of Bethlehem that was within the gate and drew water in jeopardy of their lives. Who among us would not willingly pour out his soul unto death if he might but give refreshment to the Lord? And yet He placed Himself for our sakes into a position of shame and suffering where none would wait upon Him, but when He cried, "I thirst," they gave Him vinegar to drink. Glorious humiliation of our exalted Head! O Lord Jesus, we love and worship You! We would lift Your name on high in grateful remembrance of the depths to which You descended!

While we admire His condescension, let our thoughts also turn with delight to His sure sympathy. If Jesus said, "I thirst," then He knows all our frailties and woes. The next time we are in pain or are suffering depression of spirit, we will remember that our Lord understands it all, for He has had practical, personal experience of it. Neither in torture of body nor in sadness of heart are we deserted by our Lord. His line is parallel with ours. The arrow that has lately pierced you was first stained with His blood. The cup that you are made to drink, though it is very bitter, bears the mark of His lips about its brim. He has traversed the mournful way before you, and every footprint you leave in the sodden soil is stamped side by side with His footmarks. Let the sympathy of Christ, then, be fully believed in and deeply appreciated, since He said, "I thirst."

Henceforth, let us cultivate the spirit of resignation, for we may well rejoice to carry a cross that His shoulders have borne before us. Beloved, if our Master said, "I thirst," do we expect every day to drink of streams from Lebanon? He was innocent, and yet He thirsted. Shall we marvel if guilty ones are now and then chastened? If He was so poor that His garments were stripped from

Him, and He was hung upon the tree, penniless and friendless, hungering and thirsting, will you groan and murmur because you bear the yoke of poverty and need? There is bread upon your table today, and there will be at least a cup of cold water to refresh you. You are not, therefore, so poor as He. Complain not, then. Shall the servant be above his Master or the disciple above his Lord? Let patience have her perfect work. You do suffer. Perhaps you carry about with you a gnawing disease that eats at your heart, but Jesus took our sicknesses, and His cup was more bitter than yours. Let the gasp of your Lord, "I thirst," go through your ears, and as you hear it let it touch your heart and cause you to gird up yourself and say, "Does He say, 'I thirst'? Then I will thirst with Him and not complain, I will suffer with Him and not murmur." The Redeemer's cry of "I thirst" is a solemn lesson of patience to His afflicted.

As we think of this "I thirst," which proves our Lord's humanity, let us resolve to shun no denials, but rather court them that we may be conformed to His image. May we not be half ashamed of our pleasures when *He* says, "I thirst"? May we not despise our loaded table while *He* is so neglected? Shall it ever be a hardship to be denied the satisfying draught when *He* said, "I thirst"? Shall carnal appetites be indulged and bodies pampered when Jesus cried "I thirst"? What if the bread is dry or the medicine is nauseous; yet for His thirst there was no relief but gall and vinegar, and dare we complain? For His sake we may rejoice in self-denial and accept Christ and a crust as all we desire between here and heaven. A Christian living to indulge the fleshly appetites of a brute beast, to eat and to drink almost to gluttony and drunkenness, is utterly unworthy of the name. The conquest of the appetites, the entire subjugation of the flesh must be achieved, for before our great Exemplar said, "It is finished," wherein I think He reached the greatest height of all, He stood as only upon the next lower step to that elevation and said, "I thirst." The power to suffer for another, the capacity to be self-denying even to an extreme to accomplish some great work for God—this is a thing to be sought after and must be gained before our work is done, and in this Jesus is before us our example and our strength.

Thus I have tried to spy out a measure of teaching by using that one glass for the soul's eye through which we look upon "I thirst" as the symbol of His true humanity.

## The Token of His Suffering Substitution

The great Surety says, "I thirst," because He is placed in the sinner's place, and He must therefore undergo the penalty of sin for the ungodly. "My God, my God, why hast thou forsaken me?" points to the anguish of His soul. "I thirst" expresses in part the torture of His body. And they were both needful, because it is written of the God of justice that He is "able to destroy both soul and body in hell" (Matt. 10:28), and the pangs that are due to law are of both kinds, touching both heart and flesh. See where sin begins and mark that there it ends. Sin begins with the mouth of appetite when it is sinfully gratified, and it ends when a kindred appetite is graciously denied. Our first parents plucked forbidden fruit and, by eating it slew the race. Appetite was the door of sin, and therefore in that point our Lord was put to pain. With "I thirst," the evil is destroyed and receives its expiation. I saw the other day the emblem of a serpent with its tail in its mouth, and if I carry it a little beyond the artist's intention, the symbol may set forth appetite swallowing up itself. A carnal appetite of the body, the satisfaction of the desire for food, first brought us down under the first Adam, and now the pang of thirst, the denial of what the body craved for, restores us to our place.

Nor is this all. We know from experience that the present effect of sin in every man who indulges in it is thirst of soul. Metaphorically understood, thirst is dissatisfaction—the craving of the mind for something that it does not have but that it desires. Our Lord says, "If any man thirst, let him come unto me, and drink" (John 7:37), that thirst being the result of sin in every ungodly man at this moment. Now Christ standing in the place of the ungodly suffers thirst as a type of His enduring the result of sin. More solemn still is the reflection that according to our Lord's own teaching, thirst will also be the eternal result of sin, for He says concerning the rich glutton, "In hell he lift up his eyes, being in torments," and his prayer, which was denied him, was, "Father Abraham,…send Lazarus, that he may dip the tip of his finger in water, and cool my tongue; for I am tormented in this flame" (Luke 16:23–24). Now recollect, if Jesus had not thirsted, every one of us would have thirsted forever afar off from God with an impassable gulf between us and heaven. Our sinful tongues, blistered by the fever of passion, must have burned forever had not His tongue been tormented with thirst in our place. I suppose that the "I thirst" was uttered softly, so that perhaps only one and another who stood near the cross heard it at all. It was in contrast with the louder cry of *"Lama sabachthani"* and the triumphant shout of "It is finished." But that soft, expiring sigh, "I thirst," has ended for us the thirst that otherwise, insatiably fierce, would have preyed upon us throughout eternity. O wondrous Substitution of the just for the unjust, of God for man, of the perfect Christ for us guilty, hell-deserving rebels. Let us magnify and bless our Redeemer's name.

It seems to me very wonderful that this "I thirst" should be, as it were, the clearance of it all. He had no sooner said "I thirst" and sipped the vinegar than He shouted, "It is finished!" and all was over. The battle was fought and the victory won forever, and our great Deliver's thirst was the sign of His having smitten the last foe. The flood of His grief had passed the high-water mark and began to be assuaged. The "I thirst" was the bearing of the last pang. What if I say it was the expression of the fact that His pangs had at last begun to cease and their fury had spent itself, leaving Him able to note His lesser pains? The excitement of a great struggle makes men forget thirst and faintness. It is only when all is over that they come back to themselves and note the spending of their strength. The great agony of being forsaken by God was over, and He felt faint when the strain was withdrawn. I like to think of our Lord's saying, "It is finished," directly after He had exclaimed, "I thirst," for these two voices come so naturally together. Our glorious Samson had slain His thousands, and no sooner has He thrown off the thirst than He shouted like a conqueror, "It is finished," and left the field, covered with renown. Let us exult as we see our Substitute going through with His work even to the bitter end, and then with a "Consummatum est" returning to His Father, God. O souls, burdened with sin, rest you here, and resting live.

## A Type of Man's Treatment of His Lord

It was a confirmation of the Scripture testimony with regard to man's natural enmity to God. According to modern thought, man is a very fine and noble creature, struggling to become better. He is greatly to be commended and admired, for his sin is said to be a seeking after God, and his superstition is a struggling after light. Great and worshipful being that he is, truth is to be altered for him, the gospel is to be modified to suit the tone of his various generations, and all the arrangements of the universe are to be rendered subservient to his interests. Justice must leave the field lest it be severe to so deserving a being. As for punishment, it must not be whispered to his ears polite. In fact, the tendency is to exalt man above God and give him the highest place.

But such is not the truthful estimate of man according to the Scriptures. There man is a fallen creature, with a carnal mind that cannot be reconciled to God. He is seen as worse than a brutish creature, rendering evil for good and treating his God with vile ingratitude. Alas, man is the slave and dupe of Satan and a black-hearted traitor to his God! Did not the prophecies say that man would give to his incarnate God gall to eat and vinegar to drink (Ps. 69:21)? It is done. Jesus came to save, and man denied Him hospitality. At the first there was no room for Him at the inn, and at the last there was not one cool cup of water for Him to drink. But when He thirsted they gave Him vinegar to drink. This is man's treatment of his Savior. Universal manhood, left to itself, rejects, crucifies, and mocks the Christ of God. This was the act, too, of man at his best, when he is moved to pity. For it seems clear that he who lifted up the wet sponge to the Redeemer's lips did it in compassion. I think that Roman soldier meant well, at least well for a rough warrior with his little light and knowledge. He ran and filled a sponge with vinegar. It was the best way he knew of putting a few drops of moisture to the lips of One who was suffering so much. But though he felt a degree of pity, it was such as one might show to a dog. He felt no reverence but mocked as he relieved.

We read, "The soldiers also mocked him, offering him vinegar." When our Lord cried, "Eloi, Eloi," and afterward said, "I thirst," the persons around the cross said, "Let be, let us see whether Elias will come to save Him," mocking Him. And according to Mark, he who gave the vinegar uttered much the same words. He pitied the sufferer, but he thought so little of Him that he joined in the voice of scorn. Even when man compassionates the sufferings of Christ—and man would have ceased to be human if he did not—still he scorns Him. The very cup that man gives to Jesus is at once scorn and pity, for "the tender mercies of the wicked are cruel" (Prov. 12:10). See how man at his best mingles admiration of the Savior's person with scorn of His claims: writing books to hold Him up as an example and at the same moment rejecting His deity, admitting that He was a wonderful man but denying His most sacred mission, extolling His ethical teaching and then trampling on His blood, thus giving Him drink, but that drink vinegar. Beware of praising Jesus and denying His atoning sacrifice. Beware of rendering Him homage and dishonoring His name at the same time.

Alas, I cannot say much on the score of man's cruelty to our Lord without touching myself and you. Have *we* not often given Him vinegar to drink? Did we not do so years ago before we knew Him? We used to melt when we heard about His sufferings, but we did not turn from our sins. We gave Him our tears and then grieved Him with our sins. We thought sometimes that we loved Him as we heard the story of His death, but we did not change our lives for His sake or put our trust in Him, and so we gave Him vinegar to drink. Nor does the grief end here, for have not the best works we have ever done, and the best feelings we have ever felt, and the best prayers we have ever offered, been tart and sour with sin? Can they be compared to generous wine? Are they not more like sharp vinegar? I wonder that He has ever received them, as one marvels why He received this vinegar. And yet He has received them and has smiled upon us for presenting them. He knew once how to turn water into wine, and in matchless love He has often turned our sour drink offerings into something sweet to Himself, though in themselves they have been the juice of sour grapes, sharp enough to set His teeth on edge. We may therefore come before Him with all the rest of our race, when God subdues them to repentance by His love, and look on Him whom we have pierced, and mourn for Him as one that is in bitterness for His firstborn. We may well remember our faults this day.

## The Mystical Expression of the Desire of His Heart

"I thirst." I cannot think that natural thirst was all He felt. He thirsted for water doubtless, but His soul was thirsty in a higher sense. Indeed, He seems only to have spoken that the Scriptures might be fulfilled as to the offering Him vinegar. Always was He in harmony with Himself, and His body was always expressive of His soul's cravings as well as of its own longings. "I thirst" meant that His heart was thirsting to save men. This thirst had been on Him from the earliest of His earthly days. "Wist ye not," said He, while yet a boy, "that I must be about my Father's business?" (Luke 2:49). Did He not tell His disciples, "I have a baptism to be baptized with;

and how am I straitened till it be accomplished?" (Luke 12:50). He thirsted to pluck us from between the jaws of hell, to pay our redemption price, and to set us free from the eternal condemnation that hung over us. When on the cross the work was almost done, His thirst was not assuaged and could not be till He could say, "It is finished." It is almost done, Thou Christ of God. You have almost saved Your people. There remains but one thing more, that You should actually die and hence Your strong desire to come to the end and complete Your labor. You were still straitened till the last pang was felt and the last word spoken to complete the full redemption, and hence Your cry, "I thirst."

Beloved, there is now upon our Master, and there always has been, a thirst after the love of His people. Do you not remember how that thirst of His was strong in the old days of the prophet? Call to mind His complaint in the fifth chapter of Isaiah: "Now will I sing to my well-beloved a song of my beloved touching his vineyard. My well-beloved hath a vineyard in a very fruitful hill: And he fenced it, and gathered out the stones thereof, and planted it with the choicest vine, and built a tower in the midst of it, and also made a winepress therein" (vv. 1–2). What was He looking for from His vineyard and its winepress? What but for the juice of the vine that He might be refreshed? "And he looked that it should bring forth grapes, and it brought forth wild grapes" (vs. 2)—vinegar, and not wine; sourness, and not sweetness. So He was thirsting then. According to the sacred canticle of love in the fifth chapter of the Song of Solomon, we learn that when He drank in those olden times it was in the garden of His Church that He was refreshed. What does He say? "I am come into my garden, my sister, my spouse: I have gathered my myrrh with my spice; I have eaten my honeycomb with my honey; I have drunk my wine with my milk: eat, O friends; drink, yea, drink abundantly, O beloved" (vs. 1). In the same song, He speaks of His Church and says, "The roof of thy mouth like the best wine for my beloved, that goeth down sweetly, causing the lips of those that are asleep to speak" (7:9). And yet again in the eighth chapter, the bride says, "I would cause thee to drink of spiced wine of the juice of my pomegranate" (vs. 2). Yes, He loves to be with His people. They are the garden where He walks for refreshment, and their love, their graces, are the milk and wine of which He delights to drink. Christ was always thirsty to save men and to be loved of men; and we see a type of His lifelong desire when, being weary, He sat thus on the well and said to the woman of Samaria, "Give me to drink" (John 4:7). There was a deeper meaning in His words than she dreamed of, as a verse further down fully proves, when He said to His disciples, "I have meat to eat that ye know not of" (vs. 32). He derived spiritual refreshment from the winning of that woman's heart to Himself.

And now, brethren, our blessed Lord has at this time a thirst for communion with each one of you who are His people, not because you can do Him good but because He can do you good. He thirsts to bless you and to receive your grateful love in return. He thirsts to see you looking with believing eye to His fullness and holding out your emptiness that He may supply it. He says, "Behold, I stand at the door, and knock" (Rev. 3:20). What knocks He for? It is that He may eat and drink with you, for He promises that if we open to Him He will enter in and sup with us and we with Him. He is thirsty still, you see, for our poor love, and surely we cannot deny it to Him. Come, let us pour out full flagons, until His joy is fulfilled in us.

What makes Him love us so? That I cannot tell, except His own great love. He *must* love; it is His nature. He must love His chosen whom He has once begun to love, for He is the same yesterday, today, and forever (Heb. 13:8). His great love makes Him thirst to have us much nearer than we are. He will never be satisfied till all His redeemed are beyond gunshot of the enemy. I will give you one of His thirsty prayers: "Father, I will that they also, whom thou hast given me, be with me where I am; that they may behold my glory" (John 17:24). He wants you, brother, He wants you, dear sister. He longs to have you wholly to Himself. Come to Him in prayer, come to Him in fellowship, come to Him by perfect consecration, come to Him by surrendering your whole being to the sweet mysterious influences of His Spirit. Sit at His feet with Mary, lean on His breast with John. Yea, come with the spouse in the song and say, "Let him kiss me with the kisses of his mouth: for thy love is better than wine" (Song of Sol. 1:2). He calls for that: will you not give it to Him? Are you so frozen at heart that not a cup of cold water can be melted for Jesus? Are you lukewarm? O brother, if He says, "I thirst," and you bring Him a lukewarm heart, that is worse than vinegar, for He has said, "I will spue thee out of my mouth" (Rev. 3:16). He can receive vinegar but not lukewarm love. Come, bring Him your warm heart, and let Him drink from that purified chalice as much as He wills. Let all your love be His. I know He loves to receive from you because He delights even in a cup of cold water that you give to one of His disciples. How much more will He delight in the giving of your whole self to Him? Therefore, while He thirsts, give Him to drink this day.

## The Pattern of Our Death with Him

Know you not that you are crucified together with Christ? Well, then, what means this cry, "I thirst," but that we should thirst, too? We do not thirst after the old manner wherein we were bitterly afflicted, for He has said, "Whosoever drinketh of the water that I shall give him shall never thirst" (John 4:14). But now we covet a new thirst, a refined and heavenly appetite, a craving for our Lord. O Thou blessed Master, if we are indeed nailed up to the tree with You, give us to thirst after You with a thirst that only the cup of the new covenant in Your blood can ever satisfy. Certain philosophers have said that they love the pursuit of truth even better than the knowledge of truth. I differ from them greatly, but I will say this, that next to the actual enjoyment of my Lord's presence I love to hunger and thirst after Him. Rutherford used words somewhat to this effect: "I thirst for my Lord and this is joy; a joy which no man taketh from me. Even if I may not come at Him, yet shall I be full of consolation, for it is heaven to thirst after Him, and surely He will never deny a poor soul liberty to admire Him, and adore Him, and thirst after Him."

As for myself, I would grow more and more insatiable after my divine Lord, and when I have much of Him I would still cry for more, and then for more, and still for more. My heart shall not be content till He is all in all to me, and I am altogether lost in Him. Oh, to be enlarged in soul so as to take deeper draughts of His sweet love, for our heart cannot have enough. This is a kind of sweet whereof if a man has much he must have more, and when he has more he is under a still greater necessity to receive more, and so on, his appetite forever growing by that which it feeds upon, till he is filled with all the fullness of God. "I thirst"—aye, this is my soul's word with the Lord. Borrowed from His lips it well suits my mouth.

*I thirst, but not as once I did,*
*The vain delights of earth to share;*

*Thy wounds, Emmanuel, all forbid*
*That I should seek my pleasures there.*


*Dear fountain of delight unknown!*
*No longer sink below the brim;*
*But overflow, and pour me down*
*A living and life-giving stream.*

Jesus thirsted; then let us thirst in this dry and thirsty land where there is no water. Even as the hart panteth after the water brooks, our souls would thirst after Thee, O God.

Beloved, let us thirst for the souls of our fellowmen. I have already told you that such was our Lord's mystical desire; let it be ours, also. Brother, thirst to have your children saved. Brother, thirst I pray you, to have the people at work saved. Sister, thirst for the salvation of your class, thirst for the redemption of your family, thirst for the conversion of your husband. We should all have a longing for conversions. Is it so with each one of you? If not, bestir yourselves at once. Fix your heart upon some unsaved one, and thirst until he is saved. It is the way whereby many shall be brought to Christ, when this blessed soul thirst of true Christian charity shall be upon those who are themselves saved. Remember how Paul said, "I say the truth in Christ, I lie not, my conscience also bearing me witness in the Holy Ghost, That I have great heaviness and continual sorrow in my heart. For I could wish that myself were accursed from Christ for my brethren, my kinsmen according to the flesh" (Rom. 9:1–3). Paul would have sacrificed himself to save his countrymen, so heartily did he desire their eternal welfare. Let this mind be in you, also.

As for yourselves, thirst after perfection. Hunger and thirst after righteousness, for you shall be filled. Hate sin and heartily loathe it. But thirst to be holy as God is holy, thirst to be like Christ, thirst to bring glory to His sacred name by complete conformity to His will.

May the Holy Ghost work in you the complete pattern of Christ crucified, and to Him shall be praise forever and ever. Amen.

*But lo, He comes! Gaze more intently than before. He comes who is to close the line of priests! There He stands, clothed not now with linen ephod, not with ringing bells, nor with sparkling jewels on His breastplate. But arrayed in human flesh He stands; His cross is His altar, His body and His soul the victim, Himself the priest. And lo! before His God He offers up His own soul within the veil of thick darkness that has covered Him from the sight of men. Presenting His own blood, He enters within the veil, sprinkles it there, and coming forth from the midst of the darkness, He looks down on the astonished earth and upward to expectant heaven and cries, "It is finished! It is finished!" That for which you looked so long is fully achieved and perfected forever.*

# Chapter Nine

# It Is Finished!

*When Jesus therefore had received the vinegar, he said, It is finished: and he bowed his head, and gave up the ghost*—John 19:30.

I WOULD HAVE YOU attentively observe the singular clearness, power, and quickness of the Savior's mind in the last agonies of death. When pains and groans attend the last hour, they frequently have the effect of discomposing the mind so that it is not possible for the dying man to collect his thoughts or, having collected them, to utter them so that they can be understood by others. In no case could we expect a remarkable exercise of memory or a profound judgment upon deep subjects from an expiring man. But the Redeemer's last acts were full of wisdom and prudence, although His sufferings were beyond all measure excruciating. Note how clearly He perceived the significance of every type! How plainly He could read with dying eye those divine symbols that the eyes of angels could only desire to look into! He saw the secrets that have bewildered sages and astonished seers all fulfilled in His own body. Nor must we fail to observe the power and comprehensiveness by which He grasped the chain that binds the shadowy past with the sunlit present. We must not forget the brilliance of that intelligence that threaded all the ceremonies and sacrifices on one string of thought, beheld all the prophecies as one great revelation and all the promises as the heralds of one person, and then said of the whole, "It is finished in Me." What quickness of mind was that which enabled Him to traverse all the centuries of prophecy, to penetrate the eternity of the covenant, and then to anticipate the eternal glories! And all this when He is mocked by multitudes of enemies and when His hands and feet are nailed to the cross! What force of mind must the Savior have possessed to soar above those Alps of Agony that touched the very clouds. In what a singular mental condition must He have been during the period of His crucifixion to be able to review the whole roll of inspiration!

Now, this remark may not seem to be of any great value, but I think its value lies in certain inferences that may be drawn from it. We have sometimes heard it said, "How could Christ, in so short a time, bear suffering that should be equivalent to the eternal torments of hell?" Our reply is, we are not capable of judging what the Son of God might do even in a moment, much less what He might do and what He might suffer in His life and in His death. It has been frequently affirmed by persons who have been rescued from drowning that the mind of a drowning man is singularly active. One who, after being some time in the water, was at last painfully restored, said that the whole of his history seemed to come before his mind while he was sinking and that if anyone had asked him how long he had been in the water, he should have said twenty years, whereas he had been there for only a moment or two. The intellect of mortal man is such that if God wills it, when it is in certain states, it can think out centuries of thought at once. It can go through in one instant what we should have supposed would have taken years upon years of time for it to know or feel. We think, therefore, that from the Savior's singular clearness and quickness of intellect upon the cross, it is very possible that He did in the space of two or three hours endure not only the agony that might have been contained in centuries but also an equivalent for that which might be comprehended in everlasting punishment. At any rate, it is not for us to say that it could not be so. When the Deity is arrayed in manhood, then manhood becomes omnipotent to suffer. And just as the feet of Christ were once almighty to tread the seas, so now was His whole body become almighty to dive into the great waters, to endure an immersion in unknown agonies. Do not, I pray you, attempt to measure Christ's sufferings by the finite line of your own ignorant reason, but let us know and believe that what He endured there was accepted by God as an equivalent for all our pains.

## Let Us Hear the Text and Understand It

The Son of God has been made man. He has lived a life of perfect virtue and of total self-denial. He has been all that life long despised and rejected of men, a man of sorrows and acquainted with grief. His enemies have been legion. His friends have been few, and those few faithless. He is at last delivered over into the hands of them who hate Him. He is arrested while in the act of prayer and is arraigned before both the spiritual and the temporal courts. He is robed in mockery and then unrobed in shame. He is set upon His throne in scorn and then tied to the pillar in cruelty. He is declared innocent and yet He is delivered up by the Judge who should have preserved Him from His persecutors. He is dragged through the streets of that Jerusalem that had killed the prophets and would now crimson itself with the blood of the prophets' Master. He is brought to the cross and nailed fast to the cruel wood. The sun burns Him. His cruel wounds increase the fever. God forsakes Him. "My God, my God, why hast thou forsaken me?" contains the concentrated anguish of the world.

While He hangs there in mortal conflict with sin and Satan, His heart is broken, His limbs are dislocated. Heaven fails Him, for the sun is veiled in darkness. Earth forsakes Him, for "all the disciples forsook him, and fled" (Matt. 26:56). He looks everywhere, and there is none to help. He casts His eye around, and there is no man who can share His toil. He treads the winepress alone, and of the people there is none with Him. On, on, He goes, steadily determined to drink the last dregs of the cup that must not pass from Him if His Father's will be done. At last He cries, "It is finished," and He gives up the ghost. Hear it, Christians, hear this shout of triumph as it rings today with all the freshness and force that it had centuries ago! Hear it from the sacred Word and from the Savior's lips, and may the Spirit of God open your ears that you may hear as the learned and understand what you hear!

1. What did the Savior mean when He said, "It is finished"? He meant, first of all, *that all the types, promises, and prophecies were now fully accomplished in Him.* Those who are acquainted with the original Greek will find that the words "It is finished" occur twice within three verses. In the twenty-eighth verse, the word is translated in our version "accomplished," but there it stands: "After this, Jesus knowing that all things were now *finished*, that the scripture might

be fulfilled, saith, I thirst." And then He afterward said, "It is finished." This leads us to see His meaning very clearly, that all the Scripture was now fulfilled when He said, "It is finished."

The whole book, from the first to the last, in both the law and the prophets, was finished in Him. There is not a single jewel of promise, from the first emerald that fell on the threshold of Eden to that last sapphire stone of Malachi, that was not set in the breastplate of the true High Priest. Nay, there is not a type, from the red heifer downward to the turtledove, from the hyssop upward to Solomon's temple itself, that was not fulfilled in Him. There was not a prophecy, whether spoken on Chebar's bank or on the shores of the Jordan, not a dream of wise men, whether they had received it in Babylon, or in Samaria, or in Judea, that was not now fully wrought out in Christ Jesus.

And what a wonderful thing it is, that a mass of promises and prophecies and types, apparently so heterogeneous, should all be accomplished in one Person! Take away Christ for one moment, and I will give the Old Testament to any wise man living and say to him, "Take this as a challenge. Go home and construct in your imagination an ideal character who shall exactly fit all that is herein foreshadowed. Remember, he must be a prophet like Moses and yet a champion like Joshua; he must be an Aaron and a Melchizedek; he must be both David and Solomon, Noah and Jonah, Judah and Joseph. Nay, he must not only be the lamb that was slain and the scapegoat that was not slain, the turtledove that was dipped in blood and the priest who slew the bird, but he must also be the altar, the tabernacle, the mercy seat, and the shewbread."

To puzzle this wise man further, we remind him of prophecies so apparently contradictory that one would think they never could meet in one man. "All kings shall fall down before Him: all nations shall serve Him" (Ps. 72:11); and yet, "He is despised and rejected of men" (Isa. 53:3). He must begin by showing a man born of a virgin mother: "a virgin shall conceive, and bear a son" (Isa. 7:14). He must be a man without spot or blemish but yet one upon whom the Lord shall place the iniquities of us all. He must be a glorious One, a Son of David, but yet a root out of a dry ground. Now, I say it boldly, if all the greatest intellects of all the ages could set themselves to work out this problem, to invent another key to the types and prophecies, they could not do it. I see you wise men, poring over these hieroglyphs. One suggests one key, and it opens two or three of the figures, but you cannot proceed, for the next one puts you at a nonplus. Another learned man suggests another clue, but that fails most where it is most needed, and another, and another. Thus, these wondrous hieroglyphs traced of old by Moses in the wilderness must be left unexplained, till one comes forward and proclaims, "The cross of Christ and the Son of God incarnate." Then the whole is clear, so that he who runs may read and a child may understand. Blessed Savior! In You we see everything fulfilled that God spoke of old by the prophets. In You we discover everything carried out in substance that God had set for us in the dim mist of sacrificial smoke. Glory be to Your name!

2. But the words have richer meaning. Not only were all types and prophecies and promises thus finished in Christ, but *all the typical sacrifices of the old Jewish law were now abolished as well as explained.* They were finished in Him. Will you imagine for a minute the saints in heaven looking down upon what was done on earth—Abel and his friends who had long ago before the flood been sitting in the glories above. They watch while God lights star after star in heaven. Promise after promise flashes light upon the thick darkness of earth. They see Abraham come, and they look down and wonder while they see God revealing Christ to Abraham in the person of Isaac. They gaze just as the angels do, desiring to look into the mystery. From the times of Noah, Abraham, Isaac, and Jacob, they see altars smoking, recognition of the fact that man is guilty, and the spirits before the throne say, "Lord, when will sacrifices finish? When will blood no more be shed?" The offering of bloody sacrifices soon increases. It is now carried on by men ordained for the purpose. Aaron and the high priests and the Levites, every morning and every evening offer a lamb, while great sacrifices are offered on special occasions. Bullocks groan, rams bleed, the necks of doves are wrung, and all the while the saints are crying, "O Lord, how long?" Year after year the high priest goes within the veil and sprinkles the mercy seat with blood. The next year sees him do the like, and the next, and again, and again, and again. David offers hecatombs, Solomon slaughters tens of thousands, Hezekiah offers rivers of oil, Josiah gives thousands of the fat of fed beasts, and the spirits of the just say, "Will the sacrifice never be finished? Must there always be a remembrance of sin? Will not the last High priest soon come? Not yet, not yet ye spirits

of the just, for after the captivity the slaughter of victims still remains.

But lo, He comes! Gaze more intently than before. He comes who is to close the line of priests! There He stands, clothed not now with linen ephod, not with ringing bells, nor with sparkling jewels on His breastplate. But arrayed in human flesh He stands; His cross is His altar, His body and His soul the victim, Himself the priest. And lo! before His God He offers up His own soul within the veil of thick darkness that has covered Him from the sight of men. Presenting His own blood, He enters within the veil, sprinkles it there, and coming forth from the midst of the darkness, He looks down on the astonished earth and upward to expectant heaven and cries, "*It is* finished! *It is* finished!" That for which you looked so long is fully achieved and perfected forever.

3. The Savior meant, we doubt not, that in this moment *His perfect obedience was finished.* It was necessary so that man might be saved, that the law of God should be kept, for no man can see God's face unless he is perfect in righteousness. Christ undertook to keep God's law for His people, obey its every mandate, and preserve its every statute intact. Throughout the first years of His life He privately obeyed, honoring His father and mother. During the next three years He publicly obeyed God, spending and being spent in His service, till if you would know what a man would be whose life was wholly conformed to the law of God, you may see Him in Christ.

> My dear Redeemer and my Lord,
> I read my duty in Thy word,
> But in Thy life the law appears
> Drawn out in living characters.

It needed nothing to complete the perfect virtue of life but the entire obedience of death. He who would serve God not only must be willing to give all his soul and his strength while he lives but also must stand prepared to resign life when it shall be for God's glory. Our perfect Substitute put the last stroke upon His work by dying, and therefore He claims to be absolved from further debt, for "it is finished." Yes, glorious Lamb of God, it is finished! You have been tempted in all points like as we are, yet have You sinned in none! It *was* finished, for the last arrow out of Satan's quiver had been shot at You. The last blasphemous insinuation, the last wicked temptation, had spent its fury on You. The prince of this world had surveyed You from head to foot, within and without, but he had found nothing in You. Now Your trial is over. You have finished the work that Your Father gave you to do, and so finished it that hell itself cannot accuse You of a flaw. Now, looking upon Your entire obedience, You say, "It is finished," and we Your people believe most joyously that it is even so.

Brothers and sisters, this is more than you or I could have said if Adam had never fallen. If we had been in the Garden of Eden today, we could never have boasted a finished righteousness, since a creature can never finish its obedience. As long as a creature lives, it is bound to obey, and as long as a free agent exists on earth, it would be in danger of violating the vow of its obedience. If Adam had been in paradise from the first day until now, he might fall tomorrow. Left to himself, there would be no reason why that king of nature should not yet be uncrowned. But Christ the Creator, who finished creation, has perfected redemption. God can ask no more. The law has received all it claims. The largest extent of justice cannot demand another hour's obedience. It is done; it is complete. Let us rejoice, then, in this that the Master meant by His dying cry that His perfect righteousness wherewith He covers us was finished.

4. But next, the Savior meant *that the satisfaction He rendered to the justice of God was finished.* The debt was now, to the last penny, all discharged. The atonement and propitiation were made once for all, and forever, by the one offering made in Jesus' body on the tree. There was the cup, hell was in it, the Savior drank it—not a sip and then a pause, not a draught and then a ceasing, but He drained it till there is not a dregs left for any of His people. The great ten-thonged whip of the law was worn out upon His back. There is no lash left with which to smite one for whom Jesus died. The great cannon of God's justice has exhausted all its ammunition. There is nothing left to be hurled against a child of God. Sheathed is your sword, O Justice! Silenced is your thunder, O Law! There remains nothing now of all the griefs and pains and agonies that chosen sinners should have suffered for their sins, for Christ has endured all for His own beloved, and "it is finished." Brethren, *it is more than the damned in hell can ever say.* If you and I had been constrained to make satisfaction to God's justice by being sent to hell, we never could have said, "It is finished." Christ has paid the debt that all the

torments of eternity could not have paid. Lost souls, you suffer today as you have suffered for ages past, but God's justice is not satisfied; His law is not fully magnified. And when time shall fail and eternity shall have been flying on, still forever, forever the final penny never having been paid, the chastisement for sin must fall upon unpardoned sinners. But Christ has done what all the flames of the pit could not do in all eternity. He has magnified the law and made it honorable, and now from the cross He cries, "It is finished."

5. When He said, "It is finished," *Jesus had totally destroyed the power of Satan, of sin, and of death.* The Champion had enlisted to do battle for our soul's redemption, against all our foes. He met Sin. Horrible, terrible, all but omnipotent Sin nailed Him to the cross. But in that deed, Christ nailed Sin also to the tree. There they both did hang together—Sin and Sin's Destroyer. Sin destroyed Christ, and by that destruction, Christ destroyed Sin.

Next came the second enemy, Satan. He assaulted Christ with all his hosts. Calling up his myrmidons from every corner and quarter of the universe, he said, "Awake, arise, or be forever fallen! Here is our great enemy who has sworn to bruise my head. Now let us bruise His heel!" They shot their hellish darts into His heart. They poured their boiling cauldrons on His brain. They emptied their venom into His veins. They spat their insinuations into His face. They hissed their devilish fears into His ear. He stood alone, the Lion of the tribe of Judah, hounded by all the dogs of hell. Our Champion quailed not but used His holy weapons, striking right and left with all the power of God-supported manhood. On came the hosts; volley after volley was discharged against Him. No mimic thunders were these, but such as might shake the very gates of hell. The Conqueror steadily advanced, overturning their ranks, dashing in pieces His enemies, breaking the bow and cutting the spear in sunder, and burning the chariots in the fire, while He cried, "In the name of God will I destroy you!" At last, foot to foot, He met the champion of hell, and now our David fought with Goliath. Not long was the struggle. Thick was the darkness that gathered round them both. But He who is the Son of God as well as the son of Mary knew how to smite the fiend, and He did smite him with divine fury till, having despoiled him of his armor, having quenched his fiery darts and broken his head, Jesus cried, "It is finished," and sent the fiend, bleeding and howling, down to hell. We can imagine him pursued by the eternal Savior, who exclaims:

> *Traitor!*
> *My bolt shalt find and pierce thee through,*
> *Though under hell's profoundest wave*
> *Thou div'st, to seek a shelt'ring grave.*

His thunderbolt o'ertook the fiend, and grasping him with both His hands, the Savior drew around him the great chain. The angels brought the royal chariot from on high, to whose wheels the captive fiend was bound. Lash the coursers up the everlasting hills! Spirits made perfect come forth to meet Him. Hymn the Conqueror who drags death and hell behind Him, and leads captivity captive! "Lift up your heads, O ye gates; and be ye lifted up, ye everlasting doors; and the King of glory shall come in" (Ps. 24:7). But stay; ere He enters, let Him be rid of this His burden. Lo! He takes the fiend, and hurls him down through illimitable night, broken, bruised, with his power destroyed, bereft of his crown, to lie forever howling in the pit of hell. Thus, when the Savior cried, "It is finished," He had defeated Sin and Satan, nor less had He vanquished Death.

Death had come against Him, as Christmas Evans put it, with his fiery dart that he struck right through the Savior, till the point fixed in the cross. And when he tried to pull it out again, he left the sting behind. What more could he do? He was disarmed. Then Christ set some of His prisoners free, for many of the saints arose and were seen of many. Then He said to him, "Death, I take from you your keys. You must live for a little while to be the warder of those beds in which My saints shall sleep, but give Me your keys." And lo! The Savior stands today with the keys of death hanging at His side, and He waits until the hour shall come of which no man knows. The voice of the archangel shall ring like the silver trumpets of Jubilee, and then He shall say, "Let My captives go free." Then shall the tombs be opened in virtue of Christ's death, and the very bodies of the saints shall live again in an eternity of glory.

## Let Us Hear and Wonder

Let us perceive what mighty things were effected and secured by these words, "It is finished." Thus He *ratified the covenant.* That covenant was signed and sealed before, and in all things it was ordered well, but when Christ said, "It is finished," then the

144 / *The Power of the Cross of Christ*

covenant was made doubly sure. When the blood of Christ's heart sprinkled the divine roll, then it could never be reversed, nor could one of its ordinances be broken, nor one of its stipulations fail. The covenant was on this order. God covenants on His part that He would give Christ to see of the travail of His soul; that all who were given to Him should have new hearts and right spirits; that they should be washed from sin and should enter into life through Him. Christ's side of the covenant was this: "Father, I will do Your will. I will pay the ransom to the last jot and tittle. I will give You perfect obedience and complete satisfaction." Now if this second part of the covenant had never been fulfilled, the first part would have been invalid, but when Jesus said, "It is finished," there was nothing left to be performed on His part, and now the covenant is all on one side. It is God's "I will" and "They shall." "A new heart also will I give you, and a new spirit will I put within you" (Ezek. 36:26). "Then will I sprinkle clean water upon you, and ye shall be clean" (Ezek. 36:25). "I will cleanse them from all their iniquity" (Jer. 33:8). The covenant that day was ratified.

When Christ said, "It is finished," *His Father was honored and divine justice was fully displayed.* The Father always did love His people. Do not think that Christ died to make God the Father loving. He always had loved them from before the foundation of the world, but "It is finished" took away the barriers that were in the Father's way. He would, as God of love, and now He could, as God of justice, bless poor sinners. From that day the Father is well pleased to receive sinners to His bosom. When Christ said, "It is finished," *He Himself was glorified.* Then on His head descended the all glorious crown. Then did the Father give to Him honor that He had not received before. He had honor as God, but as man He was despised and rejected. Now as God and man, Christ was made to sit down forever on His Father's throne, crowned with honor and majesty. Then, too, by "It is finished," *the Spirit was procured for us.*

> 'Tis by the merit of His death
> Who hung upon the tree,
> The Spirit is sent down to breathe
> On such dry bones as we.

Then the Spirit whom Christ had long promised perceived a new and living way by which He could come to dwell in the hearts of men, and men might come up to dwell with Him above.

That day, too, when Christ said, "It is finished," *the words had effect on heaven.* Then the walls of chrysolite stood fast. Then the jasper-light of the pearly gated city shone like the light of seven days. Before, the saints had been saved as it were on credit. They had entered heaven, God having faith in His Son Jesus. Had not Christ finished His work, surely they must have left their shining spheres and suffered in their own persons for their own sins. I might represent heaven, if my imagination might be allowed a moment, as being ready to totter if Christ had not finished His work. Its stones would have been unloosed. Massive and stupendous though its bastions are, yet had they fallen as earthly cities reel under the throes of earthquake. But Christ said, "It is finished," and oath and covenant and blood set fast the dwelling place of the redeemed, made their mansions safely and eternally their own, and bade their feet stand immovably upon the rock.

Nay, more, that word "It is finished!" took effect in the gloomy caverns and depths of hell. Then Satan bit his iron bands in rage, howling, "I am defeated by the very Man whom I thought to overcome. My hopes are blasted. Never shall an elect one come into my prison house, never a blood-bought one be found in my abode." Lost souls mourned that day, for they said, "It is finished! If Christ Himself, the Substitute, could not be permitted to go free till He had finished all His punishment, then we shall never be free." It was their double death knell, for they said, "Alas for us! Justice that would not allow the Savior to escape will never allow us to be at liberty. It is finished with Him, and therefore it shall never be finished for us." That day, too, the earth had a gleam of sunlight cast over her that she had never known before. Then her hilltops began to glisten with the rising of the sun, and though her valleys still are clothed with darkness and men wander hither and thither, groping in the noonday as in the night, yet that sun is rising, climbing still its heavenly steeps, never to set, and soon shall its rays penetrate through the thick mists and clouds. And every eye shall see Him, and every heart be made glad with His light. The words "It is finished!" consolidated heaven, shook hell, comforted earth, delighted the Father, glorified the Son, brought down the Spirit, and confirmed the everlasting covenant to all the chosen seed.

## Let Us Proclaim It

Children of God, you who by faith received Christ as your all in all, tell it every day of your lives that "it is finished." Go and tell it to those who are torturing themselves, thinking through obedience and mortification to offer satisfaction. A Hindu man is about to throw himself down upon the spikes. Stop, poor soul! Why would you bleed, for "it is finished"? Another man is holding his hand erect till the nails grow through the flesh, torturing himself with fastings and with self-denials. Cease, cease, poor wretch, from all these pains, for "it is finished!" In all parts of the earth there are those who think that the misery of the body and the soul may be an atonement for sin. Rush to them, stop them in their madness, and say to them, "Why do you do this? 'It is finished.'" All the pains that God asks, Christ has suffered. All the satisfaction by way of agony in the flesh that the law demands, Christ has already endured. "It is finished!"

When you have done this, go next to those who think by their gifts and their gold, by their prayers and their vows, by their churchgoings and their chapel goings, by their baptisms and their confirmations, by their sacrificial system, to make themselves fit for God. Say to them, "Stop, 'it is finished'; God needs not this of you. He has received enough. Why will you pin your rags to the fine linen of Christ's righteousness? Why will you add your counterfeit penny to the costly ransom that Christ has paid into the treasure house of God? Cease from your pains, your doings, your performances, for 'it is finished.' Christ has done it all." This is a thunderclap against all human righteousness. Only let this come like a two-edged sword, and your good works and your fine performances are soon cast away. "It is finished." Why improve on what is finished? Why add to that which is complete? The Bible is finished; he who adds to it shall have his name taken out of the Book of Life and out of the holy city. Christ's atonement is finished, and he who adds to that must expect the selfsame doom.

And when you shall have told it thus to the ears of men of every nation and of every tribe, tell it to all poor despairing souls. You find them on their knees, crying, "O God, what can I do to make recompense for my offenses?" Tell them, "It is finished." "O God!" they say, "how can I ever get a righteousness that is wrought out already?" They have no need to trouble themselves about adding to it if "it is finished." Go to the poor despairing wretch who has given himself up, not for death merely but for damnation. He says, "I cannot escape from sin, and I cannot be saved from its punishment." Say to him, "Sinner, the way of salvation is finished once for all." And if you meet professing Christians who are in doubt and fear, tell them, "It is finished." Why, we have hundreds and thousands who really are converted who do not know that "it is finished." They never know that they are safe. They think they have faith today but perhaps they may become unbelieving tomorrow. They do not know that "it is finished." They hope that God will accept them if they do some things, forgetting that the way of acceptance is finished. God as much accepts a sinner who only believed in Christ five minutes ago as He will a saint who has known and loved Him eighty years, for He accepts not men because of anything they do or feel but simply and only for what Christ did, and that is finished.

Oh, poor hearts! Some of you do love the Savior in a measure, but blindly. You are thinking that you must be this and attain to that, and then you may be assured of it today—if you believe in Christ, you are saved. "But I feel imperfections." Yes, but what of that? God does not regard your imperfections, but He covers them with Christ's righteousness. He sees them to remove them, but not to lay them to your charge. "Ay, but I cannot be what I would be." But what if you cannot? Yet God looks at you not as what you are in yourself but as what you are in Christ.

Come with me, poor soul, and you and I will stand together while the tempest gathers, for we are not afraid. How sharp that lightning flash, but yet we tremble not. How terrible that peal of thunder, and yet we are not alarmed. And why? Is there anything in us why we should escape? No, but we are standing beneath the cross—that precious cross which, like some noble lightning conductor in the storm, takes itself all the death from the lightning and all the fury from the tempest. We are safe. Loud may you roar, O thundering law, and terribly may you flash, O avenging justice! We can look up with calm delight to all the tumult of the elements, for we are safe beneath the cross.

Come with me again. There is a royal banquet spread. The King Himself sits at the table and angels are the servers. Let us enter. And we do enter, and we sit down and eat and drink. But how dare we do this? Our righteousnesses are as filthy rags—how could we venture to come here? Because the filthy rags are not ours any longer. We have renounced our own righteousness, and therefore we have renounced the filthy rags, and today we wear the royal garments of the Savior and are from head to foot arrayed in white, without spot or wrinkle or any such thing. We stand in the clear sunlight—loathsome in ourselves, but glorious in Him; condemned in Adam, but accepted in the Beloved. We are neither afraid nor ashamed to be with the angels of God, to talk with the glorified, nay, nor even alarmed to speak with God Himself and call Him our friend.

And now, last of all, I write this to sinners. I know not where you are, but may God find you out. You have been a drunkard, a swearer, or a thief. You have been a blackguard of the blackest kind. You have dived into the very kennel and rolled yourself in the mire. If today you feel that sin is hateful to you, believe in Him who has said, "It is finished." Let me link your hand in mine; let us come together, both of us and say, "Here are two poor naked souls, good Lord. We cannot clothe ourselves." He will give us a robe, for "it is finished." "But, Lord, is it long enough for such sinners and broad enough for such offenders?" "Yes," says He. "It is finished." "But we need washing, Lord! Is there anything that can take away black spots so hideous as ours?" "Yes," says He. "Here is the bath of blood." "But must we not add our tears to it?" "No," says He, "no, it is finished. There is enough." "And now, Lord, You have washed us, and you have clothed us, but we would be still completely clean within, so that we may never sin any more. Lord, is there a way by which this can be done? "Yes," says He. "There is the bath of water that flows from the wounded side of Christ." "And, Lord, is there enough there to wash away my guiltiness as well as my guilt?" "Aye," says He. "It is finished. Jesus Christ is made unto you sanctification as well as redemption."

Child of God, will you have Christ's finished righteousness, and will you rejoice in it more than ever you have done before? And oh, poor sinner, will you have Christ or no? "Ah," says one. "I am willing enough, but I am not worthy." He does not want any worthiness. All He asks is willingness, for you know how He puts it: "Whoever will, let him come." If He has given you willingness, you may believe in Christ's finished work. Oh, that I could "compel" you to come! Great God, make the sinner willing to be saved, for he wills to be damned and will not come unless You change his will! Eternal Spirit, source of light, and life, and grace, come down and bring the strangers home! "It is finished." Sinner, there is nothing for God to do. There is nothing for you to do. Christ need not bleed. You need not weep. God the Holy Spirit need not tarry because of your unworthiness, nor need you tarry because of your helplessness. Every stumbling block is rolled out of the road. Every gate is opened. The bars of brass are broken, the gates of iron are burst asunder. Come and welcome, come and welcome! The table is laid. The fatlings are killed. The oxen are ready. Lo! Here stands the messenger! Come from the highways and from the hedges. Come, ye vilest of the vile who hate yourselves today! Jesus calls you. Oh, will you tarry? O Spirit of God, repeat the invitation and make it an effectual call to many a heart, for Jesus' sake! Amen.

*First*, let us enjoy the high privilege of resting in God in all times of danger and pain. The doctor has just told you that you will have to undergo an operation. Say, "Father, into thy hands I commend my spirit." There is every probability that that weakness or that disease of yours will have increase upon you, and that by and by you will have to take to your bed and lie there perhaps for many a day. Then say, "Father, into thy hands I commend my spirit." Do not fret, for that will not help you. Do not fear the future, for that will not aid you. Give yourself up to the keeping of those dear hands that were pierced for you, to the love of that dear heart that was set abroach with the spear to purchase your redemption. It is wonderful what rest of spirit God can give to a man or a woman in the very worst condition. Oh, how some of the martyrs have sung at the stake! How they have rejoiced when on the rack! Bonner's coal hole at Fulham, where he shut up the martyrs, was a wretched place to lie in on a cold winter's night. But they said, "They did rouse them in the straw, as they lay in the coal-hole, with the sweetest singing out of the heaven. And when Bonner said, 'Shame on them that they should make such a noise!' they told him that he, too, would make such a noise if he was as happy as they were." When you have commended your spirit to God, then you have sweet rest in time of danger and pain.

# Chapter Ten

# Our Lord's Last
# Cry from the Cross

*And when Jesus had cried with a loud voice, he said, Father, into thy hands I commend my spirit: and having said thus, he gave up the ghost—Luke 23:46.*

THESE WERE THE DYING words of our Lord Jesus Christ: "Father, into thy hands I commend my spirit." It may be instructive if I remind you that the words of Christ upon the cross were seven. Calling each of His cries or utterances by the title of a word, we speak of the seven last words of the Lord Jesus Christ. Let me rehearse them in your hearing. The first, when they nailed Him to the cross, was, "Father, forgive them; for they know not what they do." Luke has preserved that word. Later, when one of the two thieves said to Jesus, "Lord, remember me when thou comest into thy kingdom," Jesus said to him, "Verily I say unto thee, To day shalt thou be with me in paradise." This also Luke has carefully preserved. Further on, our Lord, in His great agony, saw His mother, with breaking heart, standing by the cross and looking up to Him with unutterable love and grief. He said to her, "Woman, behold thy son!" and to the beloved disciple, "Behold thy mother!" Thus He provided a home for his mother when He Himself should be gone away. This utterance has only been preserved by John.

The fourth and central word of the seven was, "Eloi, Eloi, lama sabachthani?" which is, being interpreted, "My God, my God, why hast thou forsaken me?" This was the culmination of His grief, the central point of all His agony. That most awful word that ever fell from the lips of man, expressing the quintessence of exceeding agony, is well put forth, as though it needed three words before it and three words after it, as its bodyguard. It tells of a good man, a Son of God, *the* Son of God, forsaken of His God. That central word of the seven is found in Matthew and in Mark but not in Luke or John. The fifth word has been preserved by John; that is, "I thirst," the shortest but not quite the sharpest of all the Master's words, though under a bodily aspect perhaps the sharpest of them all. John has also treasured up another very precious saying of Jesus Christ on the cross: "It is finished." This was the wondrous word gathered up of all His lifework, for He had left nothing undone, no thread was left unraveled, the whole fabric of redemption had been woven like His garment from the top throughout, and it was finished to perfection. After He had said, "It is finished," He uttered the last word of all: "Father into thy hands I commend my spirit."

A great deal has been said by many writers about these seven cries from the cross. And though I have read what many of them have written, I cannot add anything to what they have said, since they have delighted to dwell upon these seven last cries. Here the most ancient writers, of what would be called the Catholic school, are not to be excelled, even by Protestants, in their intense devotion to every letter of our Savior's dying words. They sometimes strike out new meanings, richer and more rare than any that have occurred to the far cooler minds of modern critics, who are as a rule greatly blessed with moles' eyes, but able to see where there is nothing to be seen, but never able to see when there is anything worth seeing. Modern criticism, like modern theology, if it were put in the Garden of Eden, would not see a flower. It is like the sirocco that blasts and burns and is either dew or unction. It fact, it is the very opposite of these precious things and proves itself to be unblessed of God and unblessing to men.

Now concerning these seven cries from the cross, many authors have drawn from them lessons concerning *seven duties*. Listen, when our Lord said, "Father, forgive them," in effect He said to us, "Forgive your enemies." Even when they despitefully use you and put you to terrible pain, be ready to pardon them. Be like the sandalwood tree that perfumes the axe that fells it. Be all gentleness and kindness and love, and let this be your prayer: "Father, forgive them."

The next duty is taken from the second cry, namely, that of penitence and faith in Christ, for He said to the dying thief, "Today shalt thou be with me in paradise." Have you, like him, confessed your sin? Have you his faith and his prayerfulness? Then you shall be accepted even as he was. Learn, then, from the second cry the duty of penitence and faith.

When our Lord in the third cry said to His mother, "Woman, behold thy son!" He taught us the duty of filial love. No Christian must ever be short of love to his mother, or his father, or to any of those who are endeared to him by relationships that God has appointed for us to observe. Oh, by the dying love of Christ to His mother, let no man here unman himself by forgetting his mother! She bore you; therefore, you must bear her in her old age and lovingly cherish her even to the last.

Jesus Christ's fourth cry teaches us the duty of clinging to God and trusting in God: "My God, my God." See how, with both hands, He takes hold of Him: "My God, my God, why hast thou forsaken me?" He cannot bear to be left by God. All else causes Him but little pain compared with the anguish of being forsaken of His God. So learn to cling to God, to grip Him with a double-handed faith. If you think that He has forsaken you, cry after Him and say, "Show me why you are contending with me, for I cannot bear to be without You."

The fifth cry, "I thirst," teaches us to set a high value upon the fulfillment of God's Word. "After this, Jesus knowing that all things were now accomplished, that the scripture might be fulfilled, sayeth I thirst." Take heed in all your grief and weakness to still preserve the Word of your God and to obey the precept, learn the doctrine, and delight in the promise. As your Lord in His great anguish said, "I thirst," because it was written that so He would speak, you must regard the Word of the Lord even in little things.

That sixth cry, "It is finished," teaches us perfect obedience. Go through with your keeping of God's commandment; leave out no command, keep on obeying till you can say, "It is finished." Work your lifework, obey your Master, suffer or serve according to His will, but rest not till you can say with your Lord, "It is finished." "I have finished the work that You gavest me to do."

And that last word, "Father, into thy hands I commend my spirit," teaches us resignation. Yield all things, yield up even your spirit to God at His bidding. Stand still and make a full surrender to the Lord, and let this be your watchword from the first even to the last: "Into thy hands, my Father, I commend my spirit."

I think that this study of Christ's last words should interest you. Therefore, let me linger a little longer upon it. Those seven cries from the cross all teach us something about *the attributes and offices of our Master*. They are seven windows of agate and gates of carbuncle through which you may see Him and approach Him.

First, would you see Him as Intercessor? Then He cries, "Father, forgive them; for they know not what they do." Would you look at Him as King? Then hear His second word, "Verily I say unto thee, To day shalt thou be with me in paradise." Would you mark Him as tender Guardian? Hear Him say to Mary, "Woman, behold thy son!" and to John, "Behold thy mother!" Would you peer into the dark abyss of the agonies of His soul? Hear Him cry, "My God, my God, why hast thou forsaken me?" Would you understand the reality and the intensity of His bodily sufferings? Then hear Him say, "I thirst," for there is something exquisite in the torture of thirst when brought on by the fever of bleeding wounds. Men on the battlefield who have lost much blood are devoured with thirst and tell you that it is the worst pang of all. "I thirst," says Jesus. See the Sufferer in the body and understand how He can sympathize with you who suffer, since He suffered so much on the cross. Would you see Him as the Finisher of your salvation? Then hear His cry, *"Consummatum est"*—"It is finished." Oh, glorious note! Here you see the blessed Finisher of your faith. And would you then take one more gaze and understand how voluntary was His suffering? Then hear Him say, not as one who is robbed of life but as one who takes His soul and hands it over to the keeping of another, "Father, into thy hands I commend my spirit."

Is there not much to be learned from these cries from the cross? Surely these seven notes make a wondrous scale of music if we do but know how to listen to them. Let me run up the scale again. Here first, you have Christ's fellowship with men: "Father, forgive them." He stands side by side with sinners and tries to make an apology for them: "They know not what they do." Here is, next, His kingly power. He sets open heaven's gate to the dying thief and bids him enter. "To day shalt thou be with me in paradise." Third, behold His human relationship. How near of kin He is to us! "Woman, behold thy son!" Remember how He says, "For whosoever shall do the will of my Father which is in heaven, the same is my brother, and sister, and mother" (Matt. 12:50). He is bone of our bone and flesh of our flesh. He belongs to the human family. He is more of a man than any man.

As surely as He is very God of very God, He is also very Man of very man, taking into Himself the nature not of the Jew only but of the Gentile, too. Belonging to His own nationality but rising above all, He is the Man of men, the Son of Man.

See, next, His taking our sin. You say, "Which note is that?" Well, they are all to that effect; but this one chiefly, "My God, my God, why hast thou forsaken me?" It was because He bore our sins in His own body on the tree that He was forsaken of God. "He hath made him to be sin for us, who knew no sin" (2 Cor. 5:21), and hence the bitter cry, "Eloi, Eloi, lama sabachthani?" Behold Him, in that fifth cry, "I thirst," taking not only our sin but also our infirmity and all the suffering of our bodily nature. Then, if you would see His fullness as well as His weakness, if you would see His all-sufficiency as well as His sorrow, hear Him cry, "It is finished." What a wonderful fullness there is in that note! Redemption is all accomplished, it is all complete, it is all perfect. There is nothing left, not a drop of bitterness in the cup of gall. Jesus has drained it dry. There is not a penny to be added to the ransom price. Jesus has paid it all. Behold His fullness in the cry, "It is finished." And then, if you would see how He has reconciled us to Himself, behold Him, the Man who was made a curse for us, returning with a blessing to His Father and taking us with Him as He draws us all up by that last dear word: "Father, into thy hands I commend my spirit." Christ goes back to the Father, for "it is finished," and you and I come to the Father through His perfect work.

I have only practiced two or three tunes that can be played upon this harp of Christ's words, but it is a wonderful instrument. If it is not a harp of ten strings, it is, at any rate, an instrument of seven strings, and neither time nor eternity shall ever be able to gather all the music out of them. Those seven dying words of the ever living Christ will make melody for us in glory through all the ages of eternity.

I shall not ask your attention for a little time to the text itself: "Father, into thy hands I commend my spirit." Do you see our Lord? He is dying, and as yet, His face is toward man. His last word to man is the cry, "It is finished." Hear, all you sons of men, He speaks to you, "It is finished." Could you have a choicer word with which He should say "Adieu" to you in the hour of death? He tells you not to fear that His work is imperfect, not to tremble lest it should prove insufficient. He speaks to you and declares with His dying utterance, "It is finished." Now He has finished with you, and He turns His face the other way. His day's work is done, His more than Herculean toil is accomplished, and the great Champion is going back to His Father's throne. He speaks, but His last word is addressed to His Father: "Father, into thy hands I commend my spirit." These are His first words in going home to His Father, as "It is finished" are His last words as, for a while, He quits our company. Think of these words and may they be your first words, too, when you return to your Father! May you speak thus to your divine Father in the hour of death!

It is very noteworthy that the last words that our Lord used were quoted from the Scriptures. This sentence is taken from the thirty-first psalm, the fifth verse. What a proof it is of how full Christ was of the Bible! He was not one of those who think little of the Word of God. He was saturated with it. He was as full of Scripture as the fleece of Gideon was full of dew. He could not speak even in His death without uttering Scripture. This is how David put it: "Into thine hand I commit my spirit: thou hast redeemed me, O LORD God of truth." Now, beloved, the Savior altered this passage, or else it would not quite have suited Him. Do you see, first, He was obliged, to fit it to His own case, to add something to it? What did He add to it? Why, that word, *Father*. David said, "Into thine hand I commit my spirit." But Jesus says, "Father, into thy hands I commend my spirit." Blessed advance! He knew more than David did, for He was more the Son of God than David could be. He was *the* Son of God in a very high and special sense by eternal filiation, and so He begins the prayer with "Father." But then He takes something from it. It was needful that He should do so, for David said, "Into thine hand I commit my spirit: thou has redeemed me." Our blessed Master was not redeemed, for He was the Redeemer. He could have said, "Into thine hand I commit my spirit, for I have redeemed my people," but that He did not choose to say. He simply took that part that suited Himself and used it as His own: "Father, into thy hands I commend my spirit." Oh, you will not do better, after all, than to quote Scripture, especially in prayer. There are no prayers so good as those that are full of the Word of God. May all our speech be flavored with texts! I wish that it were more so. They laughed at our Puritan forefathers because the very names of their children were taken from passages of Scripture. But I, for my part, would much rather be laughed at for talking much of Scripture than for talking much of trashy novels.

So, then, you see how well the Savior used Scripture, and how, from His first battle with the devil in the wilderness till His last struggle with death on the cross, His weapon was ever, "It is written."

Now, I am coming to the text itself, and I am going to gather the following points from it. First, *let us learn the doctrine* of this last cry from the cross. Second, *let us practice the duty.* And third, *let us enjoy the privilege.*

## Let Us Learn the Doctrine

What is the doctrine of this last word of our Lord Jesus Christ? *God is His Father, and God is our Father.* He who Himself said, "Father," did not say for Himself, "Our Father," for the Father is Christ's Father in a higher sense than He is ours. But yet He is not more truly the Father of Christ than He is our Father if we have believed in Jesus. "For ye are all the children of God by faith in Christ Jesus" (Gal. 3:26). Jesus said to Mary Magdalene, "I ascend unto my Father, and your Father; and to my God, and your God" (John 20:17). Believe the doctrine of the Fatherhood of God to His people. Abhor the doctrine of the universal Fatherhood of God, for it is a lie and a deep deception. It stabs at the heart, first, of the doctrine of the adoption, which is taught in Scripture, for how can God adopt men if they are all His children already? In the second place, it stabs at the heart of the doctrine of regeneration, which is certainly taught in the Word of God. Now it is by regeneration and faith that we become the children of God, but how can that be if we are the children of God already? "But as many as received him, to them gave he power to become the sons of God, even to them that believe on his name: Which were born, not of blood, nor of the will of the flesh, nor of the will of man, but of God" (John 1:12–13). How can God give to men the power to become His sons if they have it already? Believe not that lie of the devil, but believe this truth of God, that Christ and all who are by living faith in Christ may rejoice in the Fatherhood of God.

Next learn this doctrine, that *in this fact lies our chief comfort.* In our hour of trouble, in our time of warfare, let us say, "Father." You notice that the first cry from the cross is like the last, the highest note is like the lowest. Jesus begins with, "Father, forgive them," and He finishes with, "Father, into thy hands I commend my spirit." To help you in a stern duty like forgiveness, cry, "Father." To help you in sore suffering and death, cry, "Father." Your main strength lies in your being truly a child of God.

Learn the next doctrine, that *dying is going home to our Father.* I said to an old friend not long ago, "Old Mr. So-and-so has gone home." I meant that he was dead. He said, "Yes, where else should he go?" I thought that was a wise question. Where else should we go? When we grow gray and our day's work is done, where should we go but home? So, when Christ has said, "It is finished," His next word, of course, is "Father." He has finished His earthly course, and now He will go home to heaven. Just as a child runs to its mother's bosom when it is tired and wants to fall asleep, so Christ says, "Father," ere He falls asleep in death.

Learn another doctrine, that if God is our Father and we regard ourselves as going home when we die, because we go to Him, then *He will receive us.* There is no hint that we can commit our spirit to God and yet that God will not have us. Remember how Stephen, beneath a shower of stones, cried, "Lord Jesus, receive my spirit" (Acts 7:59). Let us, however may we die, make this our last emotion if not our last expression: "Father, receive my spirit." Shall not our heavenly Father receive His children? If you, being evil, receive your children at nightfall when they come home to sleep, shall not your Father, who is in heaven, receive you when your day's work is done? That is the doctrine we are to learn from this last cry from the cross—the Fatherhood of God and all that comes of it to believers.

## Let Us Practice the Duty

That duty seems to me to be, first, *resignation.* Whenever anything distresses and alarms you, resign yourself to God. Say, "Father, into thy hands I commend my spirit." Sing with Faber:

> *I bow me to Thy will, O God,*
> *And all Thy ways adore;*
> *And every day I live I'll seek*
> *To please Thee more and more.*

Learn, next, the duty of *prayer.* When you are in the very anguish of pain, when you are surrounded by bitter griefs of mind as well as of body, still pray. Drop not the "Our Father." Let not your cries be addressed to the air; let not your moans be to your physician or your nurse; but cry, "Father." Does not a child so cry when he has lost its way? If it is in the dark at night, and the child alone in a room, does not it cry out, "Father." And is not a father's heart touched by that cry? Perhaps you have never cried to God and said, "Father"? Then, may my Father put love into your heart and make you say, "I will arise and go to my Father." You shall truly be known to be a son of God if that cry is in your heart and on your lips.

The next duty is the *committing of ourselves to God by faith.* Give yourself to God, trust your life with God. Every morning, when you get up, take yourself and put yourself into God's custody. Lock yourself up, as it were, in the casket of divine protection. And every night, when you have unlocked the box before you fall asleep, lock it again and give the key into the hand of Him who is able to keep you when the image of death is on your face. Before you sleep, commit yourself to God. I mean, do that when there is nothing to frighten you, when everything is going smoothly, when the wind blows softly from the south and the ship is speeding toward its desired haven. Never make yourself quiet with your own quieting. He who carves for himself will cut his fingers and get an empty plate. He who leaves God to carve for him shall often have an abundance placed before him. If you can trust, God will reward your trusting in a way that you know not as yet.

And then practice one other duty, that of *the personal and continual realization of God's presence.* "Father, into thy hands I commend my spirit." "You are here, and I know that You are. I realize that You are here in the time of sorrow and of danger. And I put myself into Your hands. Just as I would give myself to the protection of a policeman or a soldier if anyone attacked me, so do I commit myself to You. You are the unseen Guardian of the night, the unwearied Keeper of the day. You shall cover my head in the day of battle. Beneath Your wings will I trust, as a chick hides beneath the hen."

See, then, your duty. It is to resign yourself to God, pray to God, commit yourself to God, and rest in a sense of the presence of God. May the Spirit of God help you in the practice of such priceless duties as these!

## Let Us Enjoy the Privilege

First, let us enjoy the high privilege of *resting in God in all times of danger and pain.* The doctor has just told you that you will have to undergo an operation. Say, "Father, into thy hands I commend my spirit." There is every probability that that weakness or that disease of yours will have increase upon you, and that by and by you will have to take to your bed and lie there perhaps for many a day. Then say, "Father, into thy hands I commend my spirit." Do not fret, for that will not help you. Do not fear the future, for that will not aid you. Give yourself up to the keeping of those dear hands that were pierced for you, to the love of that dear heart that was set abroach with the spear to purchase your redemption. It is wonderful what rest of spirit God can give to a man or a woman in the very worst condition. Oh, how some of the martyrs have sung at the stake! How they have rejoiced when on the rack! Bonner's coal hole at Fulham, where he shut up the martyrs, was a wretched place to lie in on a cold winter's night. But they said, "They did rouse them in the straw, as they lay in the coal-hole, with the sweetest singing out of the heaven. And when Bonner said, 'Shame on them that they should make such a noise!' they told him that he, too, would make such a noise if he was as happy as they were." When you have commended your spirit to God, then you have sweet rest in time of danger and pain.

The next privilege is that of *a brave confidence in the time of death or in the fear of death.* I was led to think over this text by using it a great many times on a trip home from the church on a recent evening. The entire journey seemed like one continued sheet of fire, and the farther I went, the more vivid became the lightning flashes. But when I came at last to turn up Leigham Court Road, and the lightning seemed to come in very bars from the sky. At last, as I reached the top of the hill and a crash came of the most startling kind, down poured a torrent of hail—hailstones that I will not attempt to describe, you might think that I exaggerated. I felt that I could hardly expect to reach home alive. I was there at the very center and summit of the storm. All around me on every side and all within, it seemed like nothing but the electric fluid, and God's right arm seemed bared for war. I felt then, "Well, now I am very likely going home," and I commended my spirit to God. And from that moment, though I cannot say that I took much pleasure in the peals of thunder and the flashes of lightning, yet I felt quite as calm as I do here at this present moment. I was happy at the thought that within a single moment, I might understand more than all I could ever learn on earth and see in an instant more than I could hope to see if I lived here for a century. I could only say, "I commit myself to God. I know that I am doing my duty in going on as I am, and all is well." So I could only rejoice in the prospect of being soon with God. I was not taken home in the chariot of fire, and I was spared a little longer to go on with my life's work. But I realize the sweetness of being able to have done with it all, to have no wish, no will, no word, scarcely a prayer, but just to take one's heart up and hand it over to the great Keeper, saying, "Father, take care of me. So let me live, so let me die. I have henceforth no desire about anything. Let it be as You please. Into Your hands I commend my spirit."

This privilege is not only that of having rest in danger and confidence in the prospect of death. It is also full of *consummate joy.* Beloved, if we know how to commit ourselves into the hands of God, what a place it is for us to be in! There are the myriads of stars, there are everlasting pillars, and they do not fall. If we get into the hands of God, we get where all things rest, and we get home and happiness. We have moved out of the nothingness of the creature into the all-sufficiency of the Creator. Oh, seek to be there. Hasten to get you there, beloved friend, and live henceforth in the hands of God!

"It is finished." You have not finished, but Christ has. It is all done. What you have to do will only be to work out what He has already finished for you and show it to the sons of men in your lives. And because it is all finished, therefore say, "Now, Father, I return to You. My life henceforth shall be to be in You. My joy shall be to shrink to nothing in the presence of the All-in-All, to die into the eternal life, to sink my *ego* into Jehovah, to let my manhood, my creaturehood, live only for its Creator and manifest only the Creator's glory." O beloved, begin tomorrow morning and end tonight with, "Father, into thy hands I commend my spirit." The Lord be with you! Oh, if you have never prayed, God help you to begin to pray now, for Jesus' sake! Amen.

*Some of God's people have not yet realized this gracious fact, for still they worship afar off. Very much of prayer is to be highly commended for its reverence, but it has in it a lack of child-like confidence. I can admire the solemn and stately language of worship that recognizes the greatness of God, but it will not warm my heart or express my soul until it has also blended therewith the joyful nearness of that perfect love that casts out fear and ventures to speak with our Father in heaven as a child speaks with its father on earth. My brother, no veil remains. Why do you stand afar off and tremble like a slave? Draw near with full assurance of faith. The veil is rent. Access is free. Come boldly to the throne of grace. Jesus has brought you as close to God as even He Himself is. Though we speak of the holiest of all, even the secret place of the Most High, yet it is of this place of awe, even of this sanctuary of Jehovah, that the veil is rent. Therefore, let nothing hinder your entrance. Assuredly, no law forbids you, but infinite love invites you to draw nigh to God.*

## Chapter Eleven

# The Rent Veil

*Jesus, when he had cried again with a loud voice, yielded up the ghost. And, behold, the veil of the temple was rent in twain from the top to the bottom*—Matthew 27:50–51.

*Having therefore, brethren, boldness to enter into the holiest by the blood of Jesus, By a new and living way, which he hath consecrated for us, through the veil, that is to say, his flesh"*
—Hebrews 10:19–20.

THE DEATH OF OUR LORD Jesus Christ was appropriately surrounded by miracles. Yet it is itself so much greater a wonder than all besides that it as far exceeds them as the sun outshines the planets that surround it. It seems natural enough that the earth should quake, that tombs should be opened, and that the veil of the temple should be rent when He who only has immortality gives up the ghost. The more you think of the death of the Son of God, the more will you be amazed at it. As much as a miracle excels a common fact, so does this wonder of wonders rise above all miracles of power. That the divine Lord, even though veiled in mortal flesh, should condescend to be subject to the power of death, so as to bow His head on the cross and submit to be laid in the tomb, is among mysteries the greatest. The death of Jesus is the marvel of time and eternity, which, as Aaron's rod swallowed up all the rest, takes up into itself all lesser marvels.

Yet the rending of the veil of the temple is not a miracle to be lightly passed over. The veil was made of "fine twined linen...with cherubims of cunning work" (Exod. 26:1). This gives the idea of substantial fabric, a piece of lasting tapestry that would have endured the severest strain. No human hands could have torn that sacred covering, which could neither have been divided in the midst by any accidental cause. Yet strange to say, on the instant when the Holy Person of Jesus was rent by death, the great veil that concealed the holiest of all was "rent in twain from the top to the bottom." What did it mean? It meant much more than I can tell you now.

The rending is to be regarded as a solemn act of mourning on the part of the house of the Lord. In the East, men express their sorrow by rending their garments, and the temple, when it beheld its Master die, seemed struck with horror and rent its veil. Shocked at the sin of man, indignant at the murder of its Lord, in its sympathy it tore its holy vestment from the top to the bottom. Did not the miracle also mean that from that hour the whole system of types and shadows and ceremonies had come to an end? The ordinances of an earthly priesthood were rent with that veil. In token of the death of the ceremonial law, the soul of it gave up its sacred shrine and left its bodily tabernacle as a dead thing. The legal dispensation is over. The rent of the veil seemed to say: "Henceforth, God dwells no longer in the thick darkness of the Holy of Holies and shines forth no longer from between the cherubim. The special enclosure is broken up, and there is no inner sanctuary for the earthly high priest to enter. Typical atonements and sacrifices are at an end."

According to the explanation given in our second text, the rending of the veil chiefly meant that the way into the holiest, which was not before made manifest, was not laid open to all believers. Once in the year the high priest solemnly lifted a corner of this veil with fear and trembling, and with blood and holy incense he passed into the immediate presence of Jehovah. But the tearing of the veil laid open the secret place. The rent from top to bottom gives ample space for all to enter who are called of God's grace, to approach the throne, and to commune with the Eternal One. Upon that subject I shall try to write, praying in my inmost soul that you and I, with all other believers, may have boldness actually to enter into that which is within the veil. Oh, that the Spirit of God would lead us into the nearest fellowship that mortal men can have with the infinite Jehovah!

First, I shall ask you to consider *what has been done.* The veil has been rent. Second, we will remember *what we therefore have:* "boldness to enter into the holiest by the blood of Jesus." Then, third, we will consider *how we exercise this grace:* We "enter...by the blood of Jesus, by a new and living way, which he hath consecrated for us, through the veil, that is to say, his flesh."

## What Has Been Done

In actual historical fact, the glorious veil of the temple has been rent from the top to the bottom. As a matter of spiritual fact, which is far more important to us, *the separating legal ordinance is abolished.* There was under the law this ordinance—that no man should ever go into the holiest of all, with the one exception of the high priest, and he but once in the year and not without blood. If any man had attempted to enter there, he must have died as guilty of great presumption and of profane intrusion into the secret place of the Most High. Who could stand in the presence of Him who is a consuming fire? This ordinance of distance runs all through the law, for even the holy place, which was the vestibule of the Holy of Holies, was for the priests alone. The place of the people was one of distance. At the very first institution of the law when God descended upon Sinai, the ordinance was: "And thou shalt set bounds unto the people round about" (Exod. 19:12). There was no invitation to draw near. Not that they desired to do so, for the mountain was altogether on a smoke, and "Moses said, I exceedingly fear and quake" (Heb. 12:21). "And the LORD said unto Moses, Go down, charge the people, lest they break through unto the LORD to gaze, and many of them perish" (Exod. 19:21). If so much as a beast touch the mountain, it must be stoned or thrust through with a dart. The spirit of the old law was reverent distance. Moses, and here and there a man chosen by God, might come near to Jehovah, but as for the majority of the people, the command was, His glory at the giving of the law, we read: "When the people saw it, they removed, and stood afar off" (Exod. 20:18).

All this is ended. The precept to keep back is abrogated, and the invitation is, "Come unto me, all ye that labour and are heavy laden" (Matt. 11:28). "Let us draw near" (Heb. 10:22) is now the filial spirit of the gospel. How thankful I am for this! What a joy it is to my soul!

Some of God's people have not yet realized this gracious fact, for still they worship afar off. Very much of prayer is to be highly

166 / The Power of the Cross of Christ

commended for its reverence, but it has in it a lack of childlike confidence. I can admire the solemn and stately language of worship that recognizes the greatness of God, but it will not warm my heart or express my soul until it has also blended therewith the joyful nearness of that perfect love that casts out fear and ventures to speak with our Father in heaven as a child speaks with its father on earth. My brother, no veil remains. Why do you stand afar off and tremble like a slave? Draw near with full assurance of faith. The veil is rent. Access is free. Come boldly to the throne of grace. Jesus has brought you as close to God as even He Himself is. Though we speak of the holiest of all, even the secret place of the Most High, yet it is of this place of awe, even of this sanctuary of Jehovah, that the veil is rent. Therefore, let nothing hinder your entrance. Assuredly, no law forbids you, but infinite love invites you to draw nigh to God.

This rending of the veil signified, also, *the removal of the separating sin*. Sin is, after all, the great divider between God and man. That veil of blue and purple and fine twined linen could not really separate man from God, for He is, as to His omnipresence, not far from any one of us. Sin is a far more effectual wall of separation. It opens an abyss between the sinner and his Judge. Sin shuts out prayer and praise and every form of spiritual exercise. Sin makes God walk contrary to us because we walk contrary to Him. Sin, by separating the soul from God, causes spiritual death, which is both the effect and the penalty of transgression. How can two walk together except they be agreed? How can a holy God have fellowship with unholy creatures? Shall justice dwell with injustice? Shall perfect purity abide with the abominations of evil? No, it cannot be. Our Lord Jesus Christ put away sin by the sacrifice of Himself. He takes away the sin of the world, and so the veil is rent. By the shedding of His most precious blood we are cleansed from all sin, and that most gracious promise of the new covenant is fulfilled: "I will forgive their iniquity, and I will remember their sin no more" (Jer. 31:34). When sin is gone, the barrier is broken down, the unfathomable gulf is filled. Pardon, which removes sin, and justification, which brings righteousness, make up a deed of clearance so real and so complete that nothing now divides the sinner from his reconciled God. The Judge is now the Father. He who once must necessarily have condemned is found justly absolving and accepting. In this double sense, the veil is rent: the separating ordinance is abrogated, and the separating sin is forgiven.

Next, remember that *the separating sinfulness is also taken away through our Lord Jesus*. It is not only what we have *done* but also what we *are* that keeps us apart from God. We have sin ingrained in us. Even those who have grace dwelling in them have to complain, "When I would do good, evil is present with me" (Rom. 7:21). How can we commune with God with our eyes blinded, our ears stopped, our hearts hardened, and our sense deadened by sin? Our whole nature is tainted, poisoned, perverted by evil. How can we know the Lord? Beloved, through the death of our Lord Jesus, the covenant of grace is established with us, and its gracious provisions are on this wise: "For this is the covenant that I will make with the house of Israel after those days, saith the Lord; I will put my laws into their mind, and write them in their hearts" (Heb. 8:10). When this is the case, when the will of God is inscribed on the heart and the nature is entirely changed, then is the dividing veil that hides us from God taken away. "Blessed are the pure in heart: for they shall see God" (Matt. 5:8). Blessed are all they who love righteousness and follow after it, for they are in a way in which the Righteous One can walk in fellowship with them.

Spirits that are like God are not divided from God. Difference of nature hangs up a veil, but the new birth and the sanctification that follows upon it through the precious death of Jesus remove that veil. He who hates sin, strives after holiness, and labors to perfect it in the fear of God is in fellowship with God. It is a blessed thing when we love what God loves, when we seek what God seeks, when we are in sympathy with divine aims and are obedient to divine commands, for with such persons will the Lord dwell. When grace makes us partakers of the divine nature, then are we at one with the Lord and the veil is taken away.

"Yes," says one. "I see now how the veil is taken away in three different fashions. But God is still God, and we are but poor puny men. Between God and man there must of necessity be a separating veil caused by the great disparity between the Creator and the creature. How can the finite and the infinite commune? God is all in all, and more than all. We are nothing, and less than nothing. How can we meet?" When the Lord does come near to His favored ones, they own how incapable they are of enduring the excessive glory. Even the beloved John said, "And when I saw him, I fell at his feet as dead" (Rev. 1:17). When we have been specially conscious of the presence and working of our Lord, we have felt our

168 / *The Power of the Cross of Christ*

flesh creep and our blood chill. Then have we understood what Jacob meant when he said, "How dreadful is this place! this is none other but the house of God, and this is the gate of heaven" (Gen. 28:17). All this is true, for the Lord says, "Thou canst not see my face...and live" (Exod. 33:20), although this is a much thinner veil, and it is hard for man to be at home with God.

But *the Lord Jesus bridges the separating distance.* Behold, the blessed Son of God has come into the world and taken upon Himself our nature! "Forasmuch then as the children are partakers of flesh and blood, he also himself likewise took part of the same" (Heb. 2:14). Though He is God as God is God, yet is He as surely man as man is man. Mark well how in the person of the Lord Jesus we see God and man in the closest conceivable alliance, for they are united in one person forever. The gulf is completely filled by the fact that Jesus has gone through with us even to the bitter end, to death, even to the death of the cross. He has followed out the career of manhood even to the tomb. And thus we see that the veil, which hung between the nature of God and the nature of man, is rent in the person of our Lord Jesus Christ. We enter into the holiest of all through His flesh, which links manhood to Godhead.

Now you see what it is to have the veil taken away. Solemnly note that this avails only for believers. Those who refuse Jesus refuse the only way of access to God. God is not approachable except through the rending of the veil by the death of Jesus. There was one typical way to the mercy seat of old, and that was through the turning aside of the veil. There was no other. And there is now no other way for you to come into fellowship with God except through the rent veil, even the death of Jesus Christ, whom God has set forth to be the propitiation for sin. Come this way, and you may come freely. Refuse to come this way, and there hangs between you and God an impassable veil. Without Christ you are without God and without hope. Jesus Himself assures you, "If ye believe not that I am he, ye shall die in your sins" (John 8:24). God grant that this may not happen to you!

For believers the veil is not rolled up but rent. The veil was not unhooked and carefully folded up and put away so that it might be put in its place at some future time. Oh, no! The divine hand took it and rent it from top to bottom. It can never be hung up again, for that is impossible. Between those who are in Christ Jesus and the Great God, there will never be another separation. "Who shall separate us from the love of Christ?" (Rom. 8:35). Only one veil was made, and as that is rent, the one and only separator is destroyed. I delight to think of this. The devil himself can never divide me from God now. He may and will attempt to shut me out from God. But the worst he could do would be to hang up a rent veil. What would that avail but to exhibit his impotence? God has rent the veil, and the devil cannot mend it. There is access between a believer and his God. There must be such free access forever, since the veil is not rolled up and put on one side to be hung up again in days to come. It is rent and rendered useless.

The rent is not in one corner but in the middle, as Luke tells us. It is not a slight rent through which we may see a little, but it is rent from the top to the bottom. There is an entrance made for the greatest sinners. If there had only been a small hole cut through it, the lesser offenders might have crept through; but what an act of abounding mercy is this, that the veil is rent in the midst, and rent from top to bottom, so that the chief of sinners may find ample passage! This also shows that for believers there is no hindrance to the fullest and freest access to God. Oh, for much boldness to come where God has not only set open the door but also lifted the door from its hinges; yea, removed it, post and bar, and all!

I want you to notice that this veil, when it was rent, was rent by God, not by man. It was not the act of an irreverent mob. It was not the midnight outrage of a set of profane priests. It was the act of God alone. Nobody stood within the veil, and on the outer side of it stood the priests only fulfilling their ordinary vocation of offering sacrifice. It must have astounded them when they saw that holy place laid bare in a moment. How they fled as they saw that massive veil divided without human hand in a second of time! Who rent it? Who but God Himself? If another had done it, there might have been a mistake about it, and the mistake might need to be remedied by replacing the curtain. But if the Lord has done it, it is done rightly, it is done finally, it is done irreversibly. It is God Himself who has laid sin on Christ, and in Christ has put that sin away. God Himself has opened the gate of heaven to believers and cast up a highway along which the souls of men may travel to Him. God Himself has set the ladder between earth and heaven. Come to Him now, you humble ones. Behold, He sets before you an open door!

## What We have

"Having therefore, brethren, boldness to enter into the holiest." Observe the threefold "having" in the paragraph now before us, and be not content without the whole three. *We have "boldness to enter in."* There are degrees in boldness, but this is one of the highest. When the veil was rent, it required some boldness to *look* within. I wonder whether the priests at the altar did have the courage to gaze upon the mercy seat. I suspect that they were so struck with amazement that they fled from the altar, fearing sudden death. It requires a measure of boldness to look steadily upon the mystery of God: "which things the angels desire to look into" (1 Pet. 1:12). It is good not to look with a merely curious eye into the deep things of God. I question whether any man is able to pry into the mystery of the trinity without great risk. Some, thinking to look there with the eyes of their natural intellect, have been blinded by the light of that sun and have henceforth wandered in darkness. It needs boldness to look into the splendors of redeeming and electing love. If any did look into the holiest when the veil was rent, they were among the boldest of men. Beloved, the Holy Spirit invites you to look into the holy place and view it all with reverent eye, for it is full of teaching to you. Understand the mystery of the mercy seat, and of the ark of the covenant overlaid with gold, and of the pot of manna, and of the tables of stone, and of Aaron's rod that budded. Look, look boldly through Jesus Christ, but do not content yourself with looking! Hear what the text says: "Having boldness to *enter in.*" Blessed be God if He has taught us this sweet way of no longer looking from afar but of entering into the inmost shrine with confidence! "Boldness to enter in" is what we should have.

Let us follow the example of the high priest, and having entered, *let us perform the functions of one who enters in.* "Boldness to enter in" suggests that we act as men who are in their proper place. To stand within the veil filled the servant of God with an overpowering *sense of the divine presence.* If ever in his life he was near to God, he was certainly near to God then, when quite alone, shut in, and excluded from all the world, he had no one with him except the glorious Jehovah. O my beloved, may we enter into the holiest in this sense! Shut out from the world, let us know that the Lord is here, most near and manifest. How sweet to realize by personal enjoyment the presence of Jehovah! How cheering to feel that the

Lord of hosts is with us! We know our God to be a very present help in trouble. It is one of the greatest joys out of heaven to be able to sing—Jehovah Shammah—the Lord is here. At first we tremble in the divine presence, but as we feel more of the spirit of adoption, we draw near with sacred delight and feel so fully at home with our God that we sing with Moses: "LORD, thou hast been our dwelling place in all generations" (Ps. 90:1). Do not live as if God were as far off from you as the east is from the west. Live not far below on the earth, but live on high, as if you were in heaven. In heaven you will be with God, but on earth He will be with you. Is there much difference? He has raised us up together and made us sit together in heavenly places in Christ Jesus. Jesus has made us nigh by His precious blood. Try day by day to live in as great nearness to God as the high priest felt when he stood for a while within the secret of Jehovah's tabernacle.

The high priest had *a sense of communion with God.* He not only was near to but also spoke with God. I cannot tell what he said, but I should think that on the special day the high priest unburdened himself of the load of Israel's sin and sorrow and made known his requests unto the Lord. Aaron, standing there alone, must have been filled with memories of his own faultiness and of the idolatries and backslidings of the people. God shone upon him, and he bowed before God. He may have heard things that it was not lawful for him to utter, and other things that he could not have uttered if they had been lawful. Beloved, do you know what it is to commune with God? Words are poor vehicles for this fellowship, but what a blessed thing it is! Many of you walk with God: what bliss! Fellowship with the Most High is elevating, purifying, strengthening. Enter into it boldly. Enter into His revealed thoughts, even as He graciously enters into yours. Rise to His plans as He condescends to yours. Ask to be uplifted to Him, even as He deigns to dwell with you.

This is what the rent of the veil brings us when we have boldness to enter in. But, mark you, the rent veil brings us nothing until we have boldness to enter in. Why stand outside? Jesus brings us near, and truly our fellowship is with the Father and with His Son Jesus Christ. Let us not be slow to take up our freedom and come boldly to the throne. The high priest entered within the veil of blue and purple and scarlet and fine twined linen, with blood and with incense that he might *pray for Israel.* There he stood before the Most

High, pleading with Him to bless the people. O beloved, prayer is a divine institution, and it belongs to us. There is no fear about prayer being heard when it is offered in the holiest. The very position of the man proves that he is accepted with God. He is standing on the surest ground of acceptance, and he is so near to God that his every desire is heard. There the man is seen through and through, for he is very near to God. His thoughts are read, his tears are seen, his sighs are heard, for he has boldness to enter in. He may ask what he will, and it shall be done unto him. As the altar sanctifies the gift, so the most holy place, entered by the blood of Jesus, secures a certain answer to the prayer that is offered therein. God give us such power in prayer! It is a wonderful thing the Lord should hearken to the voice of a man, yet are there such men? Luther came out of his closet and cried, "I have conquered." He had not yet met his adversaries, but as he had prevailed with God for men, he felt that he should prevail with men for God.

But the high priest, if you recollect, after he had communed and prayed with God, *came out and blessed the people.* He put on his garments of glory and beauty, which he had laid aside when he went into the holy place, for there he stood in simple white, and nothing else. Now he came out wearing the breastplate and all his precious ornaments, and he blessed the people. That is what you will do if you have the boldness to enter into the holiest by the blood of Jesus. You will bless the people who surround you. The Lord has blessed you, and He will make you a blessing. Your ordinary conduct and conversation will be a blessed example. The words you speak for Jesus will be like a dew from the Lord. The sick will be comforted by your words. The despondent will be encouraged by your faith. The lukewarm will be recovered by your love. You will be, practically, saying to each one who knows you, "The LORD bless thee, and keep thee: The Lord make his face shine upon thee, and be gracious unto thee" (Num. 6:24–25). You will become a channel of blessing: "out of his belly shall flow rivers of living water" (John 7:38). May we each one have boldness to enter in, that we may come forth laden with benedictions!

If you will kindly look at the text, you will notice that *this boldness is well grounded.* I always like to see the apostle using a "therefore." "Having *therefore* boldness." Paul is often a true poet, but he is always a correct logician. He is as logical as if he were dealing with mathematics rather than theology. Here he writes one of his therefores.

Why is it that we have boldness? Is it not because of our relationship to Christ that makes us "brethren"? "Having therefore, *brethren*, boldness." The feeblest believer has as much right to enter into the holy place as Paul had, because he is one of the brotherhood. I remember a rhyme by John Ryland, in which he says of heaven:

> *They all shall be there, the great and the small;*
> *Poor I shall shake hands with the blessed St. Paul.*

I have no doubt we shall have such a position and such fellowship. Meanwhile, we do shake hands with him as he calls us brethren. We are brethren to one another because we are brethren to Jesus. Where we see the apostle go, we will go. Yea, rather, where we see the Great Apostle and High Priest of our profession enter, we will follow. "Having, therefore, boldness."

Beloved, we have now no fear of death in the most holy place. The high priest, whoever he might be, must always have dreaded that solemn day of atonement when he had to pass into the silent and secluded place. I cannot tell whether it is true, but I have read that there is a tradition among the Jews that a rope was fastened to the high priest's foot so that they might draw out his corpse in case he died before the Lord. I should not wonder whether their superstition devised such a thing, for it is an awful position for a man to enter into the secret dwelling of Jehovah. But we cannot die in the holy place now, since Jesus has died for us. The death of Jesus is the guarantee of the eternal life of all for whom He died. We have boldness to enter, for we shall not perish.

Our boldness arises from the perfection of His sacrifice. Read the fourteenth verse of Hebrews 10: "he hath perfected for ever them that are sanctified." We rely upon the sacrifice of Christ, believing that He was such a perfect substitute for us, that it is not possible for us to die after our Substitute has died. We must be accepted because He is accepted. We believe that the precious blood has so effectually and eternally put away sin from us that we are no longer obnoxious to the wrath of God. We may safely stand where sin must be smitten if there is any sin upon us. We are so washed, so cleansed, and so fully justified that we are accepted in the Beloved. Sin is so completely lifted from us by the vicarious sacrifice of Christ that we have boldness to enter where Jehovah Himself dwells.

Moreover, we have this for certain, that as a priest had a right to dwell near to God, we have that privilege. Jesus has made us kings and priests unto God, and all the privileges of the office come to us with the office itself. We have a mission within the holy place. We are called to enter there upon holy business, and so we have no fear of being intruders. A burglar may enter a house, but he does not enter with boldness; he is always afraid lest he should be surprised. You might enter a stranger's house without an invitation, but you would feel no boldness there. We do not enter the holiest as housebreakers or as strangers. We come in obedience to a call, to fulfill our office. When once we accept the sacrifice of Christ, we are at home with God. Where should a child be bold but in his father's house? Where should a priest stand but in the temple of his God, for whose service he is set apart? Where should a blood-washed sinner live but with his God, to whom he is reconciled?

It is a heavenly joy to feel this boldness! We have now such a love for God and such a delight in Him that it never crosses our minds that we are trespassers when we draw near to Him. We never say, "God my dread," but say "God my exceeding joy" (Ps. 43:4). His name is the music to which our lives are set. Though God be a consuming fire, we love Him as such, for He will only consume our dross, and that we desire to lose. Under no aspect is God now distasteful to us. We delight in Him, be He what He may. So you see, beloved, we have good grounds for boldness when we enter into the holiest by the blood of Jesus.

I cannot leave this point until I have reminded you that *we may have this boldness of entering in at all times*, because the veil is always rent and is never restored to its old place. "And the LORD said unto Moses, Speak unto Aaron thy brother, that he come not at all times into the holy place within the vail before the mercy seat, which is upon the ark; that he die not" (Lev. 16:2). But the Lord never says that to us. Dear child of God, you may at all times have "boldness to enter in." The veil is rent both day and night. Yea, let me say it, even when your eye of faith is dim, still enter in. When evidences are dark, still have "boldness to enter in." And even if you have unhappily sinned, remember that access is open to your penitent prayer. Come still through the rent veil, sinner as you are. Even if you have or are grieved with the sense of your wanderings, come even now! "To day, if ye will hear His voice, Harden not your hearts" (Heb. 3:7–8) but enter at once. The veil is not there to exclude you, though doubt and unbelief may make you think it is so. The veil cannot be there, for it was rent in twain from the top to the bottom.

## How We Exercise This Grace

Let us at this hour enter into the holiest. Behold the way! We come *by the way of atonement.* "Having therefore, brethren, boldness to enter into the holiest by the blood of Jesus." I have been made to feel really ill through the fierce and blasphemous words that have been used of late by gentlemen of the modern school concerning the precious blood. I will not defile my lips by a repetition of the thrice-accursed things that they have dared to utter while trampling on the blood of Jesus. Everywhere throughout this divine Book you meet with the precious blood. How can he call himself a Christian who speaks in flippant and profane language of the blood of atonement? There is no way into the holiest, even though the veil is rent, without blood. You might suppose that the high priest of old brought the blood because the veil was there, but *you* have to bring it with you though the veil is gone. The way is open, and you have boldness to enter, but not without the blood of Jesus. It would be an unholy boldness that would think of drawing near to God without the blood of the great Sacrifice. We have always to plead the atonement. As without shedding of blood there is no remission of sin, so without that blood there is no access to God.

Next, the way by which we come is *an unfailing way.* Please notice that word "by a *new* way." This means by a way that is always fresh. The original Greek suggests the idea of "newly slain." Jesus died long ago, but His death is the same now as at the moment of its occurrence. We come to God, dear friend, by a way that is always effectual with God. It never, never loses one bit of its power and freshness. The way is not worn away by long traffic: It is always new. If Jesus Christ had died yesterday, would you not feel that you could plead His merit today? Very well, you can plead that merit after these centuries with as much confidence as at the first hour. The way to God is always newly laid. In effect, the wounds of Jesus incessantly bleed our expiation. The cross is as glorious as though He were still upon it. So far as the freshness, vigor, and force of the atoning death are concerned, we come by a new way. Let it be always new to our hearts. Let the doctrine of atonement never grow stale, but let it have dew upon it for our souls.

Then the apostle adds, it is a *"living way."* A wonderful word! The way by which the high priest went into the holy place was of course a material way, and so a dead way. We come by a spiritual way, suitable to our spirits. The way could not help the high priest, but our way helps us abundantly. Jesus says, "I am the way, the truth, *and the life"* (John 14:6). When we come to God by this way, the way itself leads, guides, bears, brings us near. This way gives us life with which to come.

It is *a dedicated way:* "which he hath consecrated for us." When a new road is opened, it is set apart and dedicated for the public use. Sometimes a public building is opened by a king or a prince, and so is dedicated to its purpose. Beloved, the way to God through Jesus Christ is dedicated and ordained by Christ for the use of poor believing sinners, such as we are. He has consecrated the way toward God and dedicated it for us, that we may freely use it. Surely, if there is a road set apart for me, I may use it without fear. And the way to God and heaven through Jesus Christ is dedicated by the Savior for sinners. It is the King's highway for wayfaring men who are bound for the City of God. Therefore, let us use it. "Consecrated for us!" Blessed word!

Lastly, it is *a Christly way;* for when we come to God, we still come through His flesh. There is no coming to Jehovah except by the incarnate God. God in human flesh is our way to God. The substitutionary death of the Word made flesh is the way to the Father. There is no coming to God except by representation. Jesus represents us before God, and we come to God through Him who is our covenant head, our representative and forerunner before the throne of the Most High. Let us never try to pray without Christ, never try to sing without Christ, never try to preach without Christ. Let us perform no holy function or attempt to have fellowship with God in any shape or way except through that rent that He has made in the veil by His flesh, sanctified for us, and offered upon the cross on our behalf.

Beloved, I will finish when I have just remarked upon the next two verses, which are necessary to complete the sense. We are called to take holy freedoms with God. "Let us draw near," at once, "with a true heart in full assurance of faith" (Heb. 10:22). Let us do so boldly, for we have a great High Priest. The twenty-first verse reminds us of this. Jesus is the great Priest, and we are the sub-priests under Him, and since He bids us come near to God and He

Himself leads the way, let us follow Him into the inner sanctuary. Because He lives, we shall live also. We shall not die in the holy place unless He dies. God will not smite us unless He smites Him. So, "having an high priest over the house of God; Let us draw near with a true heart in full assurance of faith."

And then the apostle tells us that we may not come with boldness only because our high priest leads the way but because we ourselves are prepared for entrance. Two things the high priest had to do before he might enter: One was to be sprinkled with blood, and this we have; for "our hearts are sprinkled from an evil conscience" (Heb. 10:22). The other requisite for the priests was to have their "bodies washed with pure water." This we have received in symbol in our baptism and in reality in the spiritual cleansing of regeneration.

We have known the washing of water by the Word, and we have been sanctified by the Spirit of His grace. Therefore let us enter into the holiest. Why should we stay away? Hearts sprinkled with blood, bodies washed with pure water—these are the ordained preparations for acceptable entrance. Come near, beloved! May the Holy Spirit be the spirit of access to you now. Come to your God, and then abide with Him! He is your Father, your all in all. Sit down and rejoice in Him. Take your fill of love. Let not your communion be broken between here and heaven. Why should it be? Why not begin today that sweet enjoyment of perfect reconciliation and delight in God that shall go on increasing in intensity until you behold the Lord in open vision and go no more out? Heaven will bring a great change in condition, but not in our standing, if even now we stand within the veil. It will be only such a change as there is between the perfect day and the daybreak. For we have the same sun and the same light from the sun and the same privilege of walking in the light. "Until the day break, and the shadows flee away, turn, my beloved, and be thou like a roe or a young hart upon the mountains of Bether" (Song of Sol. 2:17). Amen, and Amen.

*If* you would behold the glory of God, you need not gaze between the gates of pearls; you have but to look beyond the gates of Jerusalem and see the Prince of Peace die. If you would receive the noblest conception that ever filled the human mind of the lovingkindness and the greatness and the pity, and yet the justice and the severity and the wrath of God, you need not lift up your eyes, nor cast them down, nor look to paradise, nor gaze on Tophet; you have but to look into the heart of Christ all crushed and broken and bruised, and you have seen it all. Oh, the joy that springs from the fact that God has triumphed after all! Death is not the victor; evil is not master. There are not two rival kingdoms, one governed by the God of good and the other by the God of evil. No, evil is bound, chained, and led captive. Its sinews are cut, its head is broken, its king is bound to the dread chariot of Jehovah-Jesus, and as the white horses of triumph drag the Conqueror up the everlasting hills in splendor of glory, the monsters of the pit cringe at His chariot wheels. Wherefore, beloved, I close this book with this sentence of humble yet joyful worship: "Glory be unto the Father, and to the Son, and to the Holy Ghost: as it was in the beginning, is now, and ever shall be, world without end. Amen."

# Chapter Twelve

# Mourning at the Sight of the Crucified

*And all the people that came together to that sight, beholding the things which were done, smote their breasts, and returned.*
—Luke 23:48

MANY IN THAT CROWD who came together to behold the crucifixion of Jesus were in a condition of the most furious malice. They had hounded the Savior as dogs pursue a fox, and at last, all mad with rage, they hemmed Him in for death. Others, willing enough to spend an idle hour and to gaze upon a sensational spectacle, swelled the mob until a vast assembly congregated around the little hill upon which the three crosses were raised. There unanimously, whether of malice or of wantonness, they all joined in mockery of the victim who hung upon the center cross. Some thrust out the tongue, some wagged their heads, others scoffed and jeered, some taunted Him in words, and others in signs, but all alike exulted over the defenseless man who was given as a prey to their teeth. Earth never beheld a scene in which so much unrestrained derision and expressive contempt were poured upon one man so unanimously and for so long a time. It must have been hideous to the last degree to have seen so many grinning faces and mocking eyes and to have heard so many cruel words and scornful shouts.

The spectacle was too detestable to be long endured of heaven.

Suddenly the sun, shocked at the scene, veiled his face, and for three long hours the ribald crew sat shivering in midday midnight. Meanwhile, the earth trembled beneath their feet, the rocks were rent, and the temple, in superstitious defense of whose perpetuity they had committed the murder of the just, had its holy veil rent as though by strong invisible hands. The news of this and the feeling of horror produced by the darkness and the earth tremor caused a revulsion of feelings. There were no more gibes and jests, no more thrustings out of the tongue and cruel mockeries, but they went their way solitary and alone to their homes, or in little silent groups, while each man after the manner of the Jews when struck with sudden awe smote upon his breast. Far different was the procession to the gates of Jerusalem from that march of madness that had come out therefrom. Observe the power that God has over human minds! See how He can tame the wildest and make the most malicious and proud to cower down at His feet when He does but manifest Himself in the wonders of nature! How much more cowed and terrified will they be when He makes bare His arm and comes forth in the judgments of His wrath to deal with them according to their deserts!

This sudden and memorable change in so vast a multitude is the apt representative of two other remarkable mental changes. How like it is to the gracious transformation that a sight of the cross has often worked most blessedly in the hearts of men! Many have come under the sound of the gospel resolved to scoff, but they have returned to pray. The idlest and even the basest motives have brought men under the preaching, but when Jesus has been lifted up, they have been savingly drawn to Him, and as a consequence have smitten upon their breasts in repentance and gone their way to serve the Savior whom they once blasphemed. Oh, the power, the melting, conquering, transforming power of that dear cross of Christ! My brethren, we have but to abide by the preaching of it, we have but constantly to tell abroad the matchless story, and we may expect to see the most remarkable spiritual results. We need despair of no man now that Jesus has died for sinners. With such a hammer as the doctrine of the cross, the hardest heart will be broken. With such a fire as the sweet love of Christ, the most mighty iceberg will be melted. We need never despair for the heathenish or superstitious races of men. If we can but find occasion to bring the doctrine of Christ crucified into contact with their natures, it will yet change them, and Christ will be their king.

A second and most awful change is also foretold by the incident in our text—namely, the effect that a sight of Christ enthroned will have upon the proud and obstinate, who in this life rebelled against Him. Here they fearlessly jested concerning Him and insultingly demanded, "Who is the Lord, that we should obey Him?" Here they boldly united in a conspiracy to break His bands asunder and cast His cords from them, but when they wake up at the blast of the last trumpet and see the great white throne, which, like a mirror, shall reflect their conduct upon them, what a change will be in their minds! Where then will be the quips and jests, where then the malicious speeches and persecuting words? What! Is there not one who can play the man and insult the Man of Nazareth to His face? No, not one! Like cowardly dogs, they slink away! The infidel's bragging tongue is silent! The proud spirit of the atheist is broken, his blusterings and his carpings hushed forever! With shrieks of dismay and clamorous cries of terror, they entreat the hills to cover them and the mountains to conceal them from the face of that very Man whose cross was once the subject of their scorn. Take heed, I pray you, and be changed this day by grace lest you be changed later by terror, for the heart that will not be bent by the love of Christ shall be broken by the terror of His name. If Jesus upon the cross does not save you, Christ on the throne shall damn you. If Christ dying is not your life, Christ living shall be your death. If Christ on earth is not your heaven, Christ coming from heaven shall be your hell. May God's grace work a blessed turning of face in each of us, that we may not be turned into hell in the dread day of reckoning.

I want to study the text, and in the first place, *analyze the general mourning around the cross.* Second, I shall *endeavor to join us in the sorrowful chorus.* And then, before we conclude, I shall *remind you that at the foot of the cross our sorrow must be mingled with joy.*

## The General Mourning

"All the people that came together to that sight, beholding the things which were done, smote their breasts, and returned." They all smote their breasts, but not all for the same cause. They were all afraid, but not all for the same reason. The outward manifestations were alike in the whole mass, but the grades of differences in feeling were as many as the minds in which they ruled. There were many, no doubt, who were merely moved with a transient emotion.

They had seen the death agonies of a remarkable man, and the attendant wonders had persuaded them that He was something more than an ordinary being, and therefore, they were afraid. With a kind of indefinite fear, grounded upon a lack of intelligent reasoning, they were alarmed because God was angry and had closed the eye of day upon them and made the rocks to rend. Burdened with this indistinct fear, they went their way trembling and humbled to their several homes. But perhaps before the next morning light had dawned, they had forgotten it all, and the next day found them greedy for another bloody spectacle and ready to nail another Christ to the cross, if there had been such another to be found in the land. Their beating of the breast was not a breaking of the heart. It was an April shower, a dewdrop of the morning, a hoarfrost that dissolved when the sun had risen. Like a shadow, the emotion crossed their minds, and like a shadow, it left no trace behind.

How often in the preaching of the cross has this been the only result in tens of thousands! In my own church where so many souls have been converted, many more have shed tears that have been wiped away, and the reason for their tears has been forgotten. A handkerchief has dried up their emotions. Alas! alas! alas! that while it may be difficult to move men with the story of the cross to weeping, it is even more difficult to make these emotions permanent. "I have seen something wonderful this morning," said one who had listened to a faithful and earnest preacher. "I have seen a whole congregation in tears." "Alas!" said the preacher. "There is something more wonderful still, for the most of them will go their way to forget that they ever shed a tear." Ah, shall it be always so— always so? Keep in mind that for those who do not repent there shall come to their eyes a tear that shall drip forever, a scalding drop that no mercy shall ever wipe away. It will be a thirst that shall never be abated, a worm that shall never die, and a fire that never shall be quenched. By the love you bear your souls, I pray you escape from the wrath to come!

Others among that great crowd exhibited emotion based upon more thoughtful reflection. They saw that they had shared in the murder of an innocent person. "Alas!" said they. "We see through it all now. That man was no offender. In all that we have ever heard or seen of Him, He did good, and only good. He always healed the sick, fed the hungry, and raised the dead. There is not a word of all

His teaching that is really contrary to the law of God. He was a pure and holy man. We have all been duped. Those priests have egged us on to put to death one whom it were a thousand mercies if we could restore to life again at once. Our race has killed its benefactor." "Yes," says one. "I thrust out my tongue. I found it almost impossible to restrain myself when everybody else was laughing and mocking at His tortures. But I am afraid I have mocked at the innocent, and I tremble lest the darkness that God has sent was His reprobation of my wickedness in oppressing the innocent."

Such feelings would abide, but I can suppose that they might not bring men to sincere repentance. For while they might feel sorry that they had oppressed the innocent, yet, perceiving nothing more in Jesus than mere maltreated virtue and suffering manhood, the natural emotion might soon pass away, and the moral and spiritual result be of no great value. How frequently have we seen in our hearers that same description of emotion! They have regretted that Christ should be put to death; they have felt like that old king of France who said, "I wish I had been there with ten thousand of my soldiers. I would have cut their throats sooner than they should have touched Him." But those very feelings have been evidence that they did not feel their share in the guilt as they ought to have done and that to them the cross of Jesus was no more a saving spectacle than the death of a common martyr. Dear reader, beware of making the cross to be a commonplace thing with you. Look beyond the sufferings of the innocent manhood of Jesus, and see upon the tree the atoning sacrifice of Christ, or else you look to the cross in vain.

No doubt there were a few in the crowd who smote upon their breasts because they felt, "We have put to death a prophet of God. As of old our nation slew Isaiah and put to death others of the Master's servants, so today they have nailed to the cross one of the last of the prophets, and His blood will be upon us and upon our children." Perhaps some of them said, "This man claimed to be the Messiah, and the miracles that accompanied His death prove that He was so. His life betokens it and His death declares it. What will become of our nation if we have slain the Prince of Peace! How will God visit us if we have put His prophet to death!" Such mourning was in advance of other forms. It showed a deeper thought and a clearer knowledge, and it may have been an admirable preparation for the coming of the gospel, but it would not of itself suffice as evidence of grace. I shall be glad if my readers are persuaded by the character of Christ that He must have been a prophet sent of God and that He was the Messiah promised of old. And I shall be gratified if they therefore lament the shameful cruelties that He received from our apostate race. Such emotions of conviction and pity are most commendable, and under God's blessing they may prove to be the furrows of your heart in which the gospel may take root. He who thus was cruelly put to death was God over all blessed forever, the world's Redeemer, and the Savior of such as put their trust in Him. May you accept Him today as your Deliverer, and so be saved. But if not, the most virtuous regrets concerning His death, however much they may indicate your enlightenment, will not manifest your true conversion.

In the motley company who all went home smiting on their breasts, let us hope that there were some who said, "Certainly this was the Son of God," and mourned to think He should have suffered for their transgressions and been put to grief for their iniquities. Those who came to that point were saved. Blessed were the eyes that looked upon the slaughtered Lamb in such a way as that, and happy were the hearts that there and then were broken because He was bruised and put to grief for their sakes. Beloved, aspire to this. May God's grace bring you to see in Jesus Christ no other agony, to die, the just for the unjust, that we may be saved. Come and repose your trust in Him, and then smite upon your breasts at the thought that such a victim should have been necessary for your redemption. Then may you clap your hands for very joy, for they who thus bewail the Savior may rejoice in Him, for He is theirs and they are His.

## Join in the Lamentation

We will by faith put ourselves at the foot of the little knoll of Calvary. There we see in the center between two thieves the Son of God made flesh, nailed by His hands and feet, and dying in an anguish that words cannot portray. Look steadfastly and devoutly, gazing through your tears. 'Tis He who was worshiped of angels who is now dying for the sons of men. Sit down and watch the death of death's destroyer. I shall ask you first to smite your breasts, as you remember that *you see in Him your own sins.* How great He is! That thorn-crowned head was once crowned with all the royalties of heaven and earth. He who dies there is no common man. King of kings and Lord of lords is He who hangs on yonder cross. Then see the greatness of your sins that required so vast a sacrifice. They must be infinite sins to require an infinite person to lay down His life for their removal. You can never compass or comprehend the greatness of your Lord in His essential character and dignity; neither shall you ever be able to understand the blackness and heinousness of the sin that demanded His life as an atonement.

Brother, smite your breast and say, "God be merciful to me, the greatest of sinners, for I am such." Look well into the face of Jesus and see how vile they have made Him! They have stained those cheeks with spittle; they have lashed those shoulders with a felon's scourge. They have put Him to the death that was only awarded to the meanest Roman slave. They have hung Him up between heaven and earth, as though He were fit for neither. They have stripped Him naked and left Him not a rag to cover Him! See here then, O believer, the shame of your sins. What a shameful thing your sin must have been. What a disgraceful and abominable thing, if Christ must be made such a shame for you! Be ashamed of yourself to think your Lord should thus be scorned and made nothing of for you! See how they aggravate His sorrows! It was not enough to crucify Him; they must insult Him. And that was not enough; they must mock His prayers and turn His dying cries into themes for jest while they offer Him vinegar to drink. See, beloved, how aggravated were your sins and mine! Come, let us both smite upon our breasts and say, "Oh, how our sins have piled upon their guiltiness! It was not merely that we broke the law, but we sinned against light and knowledge, against rebukes and warnings. As His griefs are aggravated, even so are our sins!"

Look still into His dear face and see the lines of anguish that indicate the deeper inward sorrow that far transcends mere bodily pain and agony. God, His Father, has forsaken Him. God has made Him a curse for us. Then what must the curse of God have been against us? What must our sins have deserved? If, when sin was only imputed to Christ and laid upon Him for a while, His Father turned His head away and made His Son cry out, "Lama Sabachthani!" What an accursed thing our sin must be, and what a curse would have come upon us. What thunderbolts, what coals of fire, what indignation, and wrath from the Most High must have been our portion had not Jesus interposed! If Jehovah did not spare His Son, how little would He have spared guilty, worthless men if He had dealt with us after our sins and rewarded us according to our iniquities!

As we still sit down and look at Jesus, we remember that His death was voluntary—He need not have died unless He had so willed. Here then is another striking feature of our sin, for our sin was voluntary, too. We did not sin as of compulsion, but we deliberately chose the evil way. Let both of us sit down together and tell the Lord that we have no justification or extenuation or excuse to offer. We have sinned willfully against light and knowledge, against love and mercy. Let us smite upon our breasts, as we see Jesus willingly suffer, and confess that we have willingly offended against the just and righteous laws of a most good and gracious God. I could desire to keep you looking into those five wounds and studying that marred face and counting every purple drop that flowed from His hands and feet and side, but time would fail us. Only that one wound—let it abide with you—smite your breast because you see in Christ your sin.

Looking again—changing, as it were, our standpoint but still keeping our eye upon the same dear crucified One, let us see there *the neglected and despised remedy for our sin*. If sin itself, in its first condition, as rebellion, bring no tears to our eyes, it certainly should in its second manifestation, as ingratitude. The sin of rebellion is vile, but the sin of slighting the Savior is viler still. He who hangs on the tree, in groans and griefs unutterable, is He whom some of us have never thought of, whom we do not love, to whom we never pray, in whom we place no confidence, and whom we never serve. I will not accuse you, but I will ask those dear wounds to do it, sweetly and tenderly. I will rather accuse myself, for alas! alas! there was a time when I heard of Him as with a deaf ear. I was told of Jesus and understood the love He bore to sinners, and yet my heart was like a stone within me and would not be moved. I closed my ear and would not be charmed, even with such a master fascination as the disinterested love of Jesus. I think if I had been spared to live the life of an ungodly man for thirty, forty, or fifty years and had been converted at last, I should never have been able to blame myself sufficiently for rejecting Jesus during all those years. Why, even those of us who were converted in our youth and childhood cannot help blaming ourselves to think that so dear a friend, who had done so much for us, was so long slighted by us. Who could have done more for us than He, since He gave Himself for our sins? Ah, how did we wrong Him while we withheld our hearts from Him! How can we keep the doors of our hearts shut against the friend of sinners? How can we close the door against Him who cries, "Open to me,…my love,…for my head is filled with dew, and my locks with the drops of the night" (Song of Sol. 5:2)?

I am persuaded there are some readers who were chosen by Jesus from before the foundation of the world, and you shall be with Him in heaven one day to sing His praises. And yet, at this moment, though you hear His name, you do not love Him, and though you are told of what He did, you do not trust Him. What! Shall that iron bar always fast close the gate of your heart? Shall that door still be always bolted? O Spirit of the living God, win an entrance for the blessed Christ! If anything can do it, surely it must be a sight of the crucified Christ. That matchless spectacle shall make a heart of stone relent and melt, by Jesus' love subdued. May the Holy Ghost work this gracious melting, and He shall have all the honor.

Still keeping you at the foot of the cross, dear friend, every believer here may well smite upon his breast as he thinks of *who it was upon the cross.* Who was it? It was He who loved us before the world was made. It was He who is this day the Bridegroom of our souls, our Best-loved. It was He who has taken us into the banqueting house and waved His banner of love over us. He has made us one with Himself and has vowed to present us to His Father without spot. It is He, our Husband, our Ishi, who has called us His Hephzibah because His soul delights in us. It is He who suffered thus for us. Suffering does not always excite the same degree of pity. You must know something of the individual before the innermost depths of the soul are stirred. And so it happens to us that the higher the character and the more able we are to appreciate it, the closer the relation and the more fondly we reciprocate the love, the more deeply does suffering strike the soul. Sit you down and smite your breasts that *He* should grieve, that heaven's Sun should be eclipsed, that heaven's Lily should be spotted with blood, and heaven's Rose should be whitened with a deadly pallor. Lament that perfection should be accused, innocence smitten, and love murdered, and that Christ, the happy and the holy, the ever blessed, who had been for ages the delight of angels, should now become the sorrowful, the acquaintance of grief, the bleeding, and the dying. Smite upon your breasts, believers, and go your way!

Beloved in the Lord, if such grief as this should be kindled in you, it will be well to pursue the subject and to reflect upon how unbelieving and how cruel we have been to Jesus since the day that we have known Him. What, does He bleed for me, and have I doubted Him? Is He the Son of God, and have I suspected his fidelity? Have I stood at the foot of the cross unmoved? Have I spoken of my dying Lord in a cold, indifferent spirit? Have I ever preached Christ crucified with a dry eye and a heart unmoved? Do I bow my knee in private prayer, and are my thoughts wandering when they should be bound hand and foot to His dear bleeding self? Am I accustomed to turn over the pages of the evangelists that record my Master's wondrous sacrifice, and have I never stained those pages with my tears? Have I never paused spellbound over the sacred sentence that recorded this miracle of miracles, this marvel of marvels? Oh, shame upon you, hard heart! Well may I smite you. May God smite you with the hammer of His Spirit and break you to pieces. Oh, you stony heart, you granite soul, you flinty spirit, well may I strike the breast that harbors you, to think that I should be so doltish in the presence of love so amazing, so divine.

Brethren, you may smite upon your breasts as you look at the cross and mourn that you should have done so little for your Lord. What! Am I really pardoned? Am I in very deed washed in that warm stream that gushed from the riven side of Jesus, and yet am I not wholly consecrated to Christ? What! In my body do I bear the marks of the Lord Jesus, and can I live almost without a thought of Him? Am I plucked like a brand from the burning, and have I small care to win others from the wrath to come? Has Jesus stooped to win me, and do I not labor to win others for Him? Was He all in earnest about me, and am I only half in earnest about Him? Dare I waste a minute, dare I trifle away an hour? Have I an evening to spend in vain gossip and idle frivolities? O my heart, well may I smite you that at the sight of the death of the dear Lover of my soul I should not be fired by the highest zeal and be impelled by the most ardent love to a perfect consecration of every power of my nature, every affection of my spirit, every faculty of my whole man. This mournful strain might be pursued to far greater lengths. We might follow up our confessions, still smiting, still accusing, still regretting, still bewailing. We might continue upon the bass notes evermore, and yet might we not express sufficient contrition for the shameful manner in which we have treated our blessed Friend. We might say with one of our hymn writers:

*Lord, let me weep for nought but sin,*
*And after none but Thee;*
*And then I would—O that I might—*
*A constant weeper be!*

## At Calvary, Mournful Notes
## Are Not the Only Suitable Music

We admired the poet when, in a hymn that we sing at our church, he appears to question with himself which would be the most fitting tune for Golgotha:

*"It is finished"; shall we raise*
*Songs of sorrow or of praise?*
*Mourn to see the Savior die,*
*Or proclaim his victory?*

*If of Calvary we tell,*
*How can songs of triumph swell?*
*If of man redeemed from woe,*
*How shall notes of mourning flow?*

He shows that since our sin pierced the side of Jesus, there is cause for unlimited lamentation, but since the blood that flowed from the wound has cleansed our sin, there is ground for unbounded thanksgiving. Therefore, the poet, after having balanced the matter in a few verses, concludes with:

*"It is finished," let us raise*
*Songs of thankfulness and praise.*

After all, you and I are not in the same condition as the multitude who had surrounded Calvary. At that time our Lord was still dead, but now He is risen indeed. There were yet three days in which Jesus must dwell in the regions of the dead. Our Lord, therefore, so far as human eyes could see Him, was a proper object of pity and mourning and not of thanksgiving. But now, beloved, He ever lives and gloriously reigns. No vault for the dead confines that blessed body. He saw no corruption, for the moment when the third day dawned, He could no longer be held with the bonds of death, but He manifested Himself alive unto His disciples. He tarried in this world for forty days. Some of His time was spent with those who knew Him in the flesh. Perhaps a larger part of it was passed with those saints who came out of their graves after His resurrection. But certain it is that He is gone up, as the firstfruit from the dead. He is gone up to the right hand of God, even the Father. Do not bewail those wounds; they are lustrous with supernal splendor. Do not lament His death: He lives no more to die. Do not mourn that shame and spitting:

> *The head that once was crowned with thorns,*
> *Is crowned with glory now.*

Look up and thank God that death has no more dominion over Him. He ever lives to make intercession for us, and He shall shortly come with angelic bands surrounding Him to judge the quick and the dead. The argument for joy overshadows the reason for sorrow. Like as a woman when the manchild is born remembers no more her anguish, for joy that a man is born into the world, so, in the thought of the risen Savior, who has taken possession of His crown, we will forget the lamentation of the cross and the sorrows of the broken heart of Calvary.

Moreover, hear ye the shrill voice of the high-sounding cymbals and let your hearts rejoice within you, for in His death our Redeemer conquered all the hosts of hell. They came against Him furiously, yea, they came against Him to eat up His flesh, but they stumbled and fell. They compassed Him about, yea, they compassed Him about like bees, but in the name of the Lord does the Champion destroy them. Against the whole multitude of sins and all the battalions of the pit, the Savior stood, a solitary soldier fighting against innumerable bands, but He has slain them all. "Bruised is the dragon's head." Jesus has led captivity captive. He conquered when He fell, and He let the notes of victory drown forever the cries of sorrow.

Moreover, brethren, let it be remembered that men have been saved. Let the innumerable company of the elect stream before your gladdened eyes. Robed in white they come in long procession from distant lands. Once scarlet with sin and black with iniquity, they are all white and pure and without spot before the throne forever, beyond temptation, beautified, and made like to Jesus. And how? It was all through Calvary. There was their sin put away. There was their everlasting righteousness brought in and consummated. Let the hosts that are before the throne, as they wave their palms and touch their golden harps, excite you to a joy like their own, and let that celestial music hush the gentler voices that mournfully exclaim:

> *Alas! and did my Saviour bleed?*
> *And did my Sovereign die?*
> *Would He devote that sacred head*
> *For such a worm as I?*

Nor is that all. You yourself are saved. O brother, this will always be one of your greatest joys. That others are converted through your instrumentality is occasion for much thanksgiving, but your Savior's advice to you is, "Notwithstanding in this rejoice not, that the spirits are subject unto you; but rather rejoice, because your names are written in heaven" (Luke 10:20). You, a spirit deserving to be cast away, you whose portion must have been with devils—*you* are this day forgiven, adopted, saved, on the road to heaven. Oh, while you think that you are saved from hell, that you are lifted up to glory, you cannot but rejoice that your sin is put away from you through the death of Jesus Christ, your Lord!

Lastly, there is one thing for which we should always remember Christ's death with joy, and that is that although the crucifixion of Jesus was intended to be a blow at the honor and glory of our God, yet never did God have such honor and glory as He obtained through the sufferings of Jesus. Oh, they thought to scorn Him, but they lifted His name on high! They thought that God was dishonored when He was most glorified. The image of the invisible, had they not marred it? The express image of the Father's person, had they not defiled it? Ah, so they said! But He who sits in the heavens may well laugh and have them in derision, for what did they? They did but break the alabaster box, and all the blessed drops of infinite mercy streamed forth to perfume all words. They did but rend the veil, and then the glory that had been hidden between the cherubim shone forth upon all lands. O nature, adoring God with your ancient and priestly mountains, extolling Him with your trees that clap their hands, and worshiping with thy seas that in their fullness roar out Jehovah's praise, with all your tempests and flames of fire, your dragons and your deeps, the snow and your hail, you cannot glorify God as Jesus glorified Him when He became obedient unto death. O heaven, with all your jubilant angels, your ever chanting cherubim and seraphim, your thrice holy hymns, your streets of gold and endless harmonies, you cannot reveal the Deity as Jesus Christ revealed it on the cross. O hell, with all your infinite horrors and flames unquenchable and pains and griefs and shrieks of tortured ghosts, even you cannot reveal the justice of God as Christ revealed it in His riven heart upon the bloody tree.

O earth and heaven and hell! O time and eternity, things present and things to come, visible and invisible, you are dim mirrors of the Godhead compared with the bleeding Lamb. O heart of God, I see you nowhere as at Golgotha, where the Word incarnate reveals the justice and the love, the holiness and the tenderness of God in one blaze of glory. If any created mind desires to see the glory of God, he need not gaze upon the starry skies or soar into the heaven of heavens; he has but to bow at the foot of the cross and watch the crimson streams that gush from Immanuel's wounds.

If you would behold the glory of God, you need not gaze between the gates of pearls; you have but to look beyond the gates of Jerusalem and see the Prince of Peace die. If you would receive the noblest conception that ever filled the human mind of the lovingkindness and the greatness and the pity, and yet the justice and the severity and the wrath of God, you need not lift up your eyes, nor cast them down, nor look to paradise, nor gaze on Tophet; you have but to look into the heart of Christ all crushed and broken and bruised, and you have seen it all. Oh, the joy that springs from the fact that God has triumphed after all! Death is not the victor; evil is not master. There are not two rival kingdoms, one governed by the God of good and the other by the God of evil. No, evil is bound, chained, and led captive. Its sinews are cut, its head is broken, its king is bound to the dread chariot of Jehovah-Jesus, and as the white horses of triumph drag the Conqueror up the everlasting hills in splendor of glory, the monsters of the pit cringe at His chariot wheels. Wherefore, beloved, I close this book with this sentence of humble yet joyful worship: "Glory be unto the Father, and to the Son, and to the Holy Ghost: as it was in the beginning, is now, and ever shall be, world without end. Amen."